ANGER MANAGEMENT WORKBOOK
FOR TEENS

**Exercises and Tools to Overcome
Your Anger and Manage Your Emotions**

Holly Forman-Patel, MA, LMFT, LPCC

ROCKRIDGE
PRESS

For general information on our other products and services or to obtain technical support, please contact our Customer Care Department within the United States at (866) 744-2665, or outside the United States at (510) 253-0500.

Rockridge Press publishes its books in a variety of electronic and print formats. Some content that appears in print may not be available in electronic books, and vice versa.

Interior and Cover Designer: Heather Krakora
Art Producer: Janice Ackerman
Editor: Laura Apperson
Production Editor: Jenna Dutton
Production Manager: Holly Haydash

Illustration: Courtesy of istock

Paperback ISBN: 978-1-64876-794-4
R0

CONTENTS

INTRODUCTION

HELLO, YOU!

My name is Holly Forman-Patel, and I am a marriage and family therapist and professional clinical counselor. I want to welcome you and thank you for making the decision to open this workbook!

I have worked with teens for more than a decade with the challenges they face, from stress to anxiety to trauma and, as you might have guessed, anger. Anger is one of the most challenging things we can experience. But I can tell you that anyone can make shifts with their experience of anger that will help them lead a happy and fulfilling life.

I know this for two reasons: The first is because I have experienced the intense power of anger personally and had to figure out ways to manage it when I was younger. And second is that I have witnessed the amazing transformation away from anger that so many of the teens I have worked with have been able to accomplish. They went from being controlled by anger to understanding their triggers and using what they know to channel anger into something more helpful.

I am so excited to be able to share the tools that have helped so many others.

Change is HARD. It can be scary, uncomfortable, and a lot of work. It's so hard when we (or those around us) notice that something about us, like our anger, is beginning to have a negative impact on our life. Anger can feel very exhausting and take up a lot of space. This doesn't have to be your way of life—through this book, you'll find strategies to feel less impacted by anger.

You are not the first teen, nor will you be the last, to need some extra skills to manage anger. A lot of adults need this help, too! But why put off something that can help you live an easier and fuller life when you can do this now? The positive shifts I have seen in teens who learn the skills in this book are huge. They range from healthier friendships and romantic relationships to getting in trouble less often and having less conflict in their lives to feeling better about themselves and more hopeful about their future.

In addition to teaching skills to manage anger, this book will help you identify what might be fueling the anger. It'll also allow you to see that you're not alone—this struggle is happening not just for you but for many other teens as well.

This workbook contains three main parts. The first will talk more about anger, its impact, and the science behind it (what's going on in your body). The second part will introduce you to common situations involving anger that other teens have experienced and their solutions. Lastly, the third part dives into very specific situations with a focus on real-life questions and experiences teens have had and strategies to address them.

The exercises in this book come from a variety of evidence-based therapies, which means they are found through research to be effective treatments. These therapies include cognitive behavioral therapy, mindfulness, Eye Movement Desensitization and Reprocessing (EMDR) Therapy, dialectical behavior therapy (DBT), and more. You don't need to know how they work, just that they *do* work!

My hope for you is that you start this book with an open mind and kindness for yourself. You're lovely and deserving, and now you're on the path to creating some amazing changes in your life.

FIRST THINGS FIRST: THE FACTS ABOUT ANGER

Anger is a fantastic emotion! Your reaction to that might be: *Huh?* No, really, it's wonderful. It prompts us to take action. It lets us know that something needs to change. Let's just take a moment to thank our anger for trying to help us out.

Now the challenge: Anger can sometimes come out in hurtful ways. Anger is NOT bad. It's GOOD. We do not need to feel bad about ourselves for becoming angry or even if we have used anger in a hurtful way. However, we are responsible for our actions, including perhaps needing to make amends and apologize. Mistakes happen, and the hard part is that we can't take them back or change the past. The important thing is for us to learn why we made the mistake and then make a change so it doesn't happen again. When we use anger as a guide to help us, we can learn so much about ourselves, including ways to live our best life.

But what does this mean—*living our best life*? Well, as we grow older, we want to become awesome adults, so our goal is to use anger to help and guide us as opposed to letting it control us.

By beginning to understand WHY you are angry, you'll begin to learn ways to respond to other feelings that might be fueling anger, and as a result, you'll be able to manage anger in more helpful ways.

You have taken a step in a positive direction, and I am so excited to be on this journey with you. Let's go!

WHAT IS ANGER?

Being a teen is HARD.

I am not just saying this as an adult who is trying to connect with you (though I do hope this happens!). I really get it. You are being told what to do much of the time. You are expected to be responsible yet not given many of the responsibilities that you truly want. There are things outside your control that highly impact you and that you cannot yet change. This can lead to a lot of frustration and anger.

Anger is absolutely a normal emotion. You are not strange, weird, from outer space, or messed up if you are angry. Feeling anger is helpful and good because it lets us know that something is happening inside or around us that needs to be dealt with.

Anger is a surface emotion. This means that anger can sometimes be covering up a different feeling. Feelings that anger might be hiding include anxiety, sadness, hurt, and shame. The skills in this book are meant to help you discover what feelings exist underneath your anger so you can deal with them, too.

Anger can show up in a variety of ways. Some people show their anger with outward behaviors, such as yelling, becoming physical, blaming others, ignoring requests from adults, or just being mean. Others turn their anger internally, meaning they might have negative thoughts about themselves, isolate from other people, or feel sad a lot of the time.

These different responses are often related to the body's fight-or-flight response. You know that feeling when something really angers you and your body goes on alert and you feel tension and adrenaline rushing through your body? Here's what happens: When a person becomes angry, this activates the part of the brain called the *amygdala*, which then sends signals to other parts of the brain, telling it that a threat is present. When this happens, the part of the brain that helps the other parts of the brain work together can't do its job. This is why people who struggle with anger have a hard time "in the moment" shifting away from anger once that fight-or-flight response is activated. You'll learn skills in this book to help manage this situation.

Another good reason to work on anger issues: There is a connection between anger and chronic (long-term) health issues. First, since anger causes the body to be very alert (known as *hyperarousal* and *hypervigilance*), over time, this can affect the immune system and heart health in a negative way. Also, if you are already struggling with other emotional issues, such as depression, anxiety, or panic attacks, anger can make them harder to manage.

Learning to manage anger can be hard at first, but it's so important. We can feel overwhelmed by anger but then deal with it in ways that hurt us or those around us. When anger is left unmanaged, you are more likely to engage in impulsive behaviors or overreact to situations that didn't really require as big a reaction—these kinds of reactions can have really unwanted consequences. You might alienate friends, lose privileges you have earned (like a cell phone or later curfew on weekends), and end up feeling not so great about yourself.

But anger is not here to hurt us; it's here to help and guide. We can learn how to take advantage of what it's teaching us.

What Anger Is Not

There is a good chance that you might have learned some incorrect information about anger over the years. Let's review some common misinformation.

MYTH	TRUTH
Anger is bad.	Anger is not bad. It is not something to fear. It's something to embrace and use as a tool. A common belief is that if we allow ourselves to express or feel our anger, we will not be able to control ourselves and will not be successful in life. Ironically, this might actually happen when we pretend we are not angry or when we allow our anger to take over. If we avoid our anger, pretend it's not there, and don't allow ourselves to feel it until it's bursting out of us, then anger will most likely come out in surprising ways that are hurtful and not helpful. Feeling our anger, understanding what is causing it, and learning helpful ways to express it will allow us to take back control.
Anger is someone else's fault.	We do not cause our anger, yet being angry is not a reason to behave in ways that hurt us or others. Anger is NOT uncontrollable, nor is it someone else's fault. It can be very easy to want to blame our anger on the actions of someone else. Yes, someone might do something that we perceive as a threat, triggers our anger, or isn't very nice; however, if we choose to respond by breaking something or hurting someone, it is then on us, not the other person.
Anger makes us powerful or gives us control back.	Anger does not always make us powerful, even though it may feel that way. Sometimes, when we feel threatened or like something is unfair, we feel powerless or not in control. Anger can sometimes trick us into thinking that we can take this control back by yelling, hitting, seeking revenge, and so on. However, in these situations, anger is in control, not us. Anger can give us power when we use it in a controlled way, such as when we are inspired by anger to take action to right a wrong in a positive way. For example, if we feel that someone is being mistreated, anger can prompt us to step in and help or inspire us to find ways to make sure the same thing doesn't happen again.

In any case, the best ways to respond to anger are to NOTICE the anger. FEEL the anger. CHANNEL the anger to be helpful and not hurtful. BE the awesome you who you are.

Check In with Yourself

There are many different ways to express anger, in both healthy and unhealthy ways. For each of the following sections, look over the statements, beliefs, and ways we can manage anger. Check off the ones you experience or believe or that apply to you. A few blank lines are included for you to fill in your own ideas.

HEALTHY ANGER EXPRESSION

☐ I talk about what is bothering me.

☐ I address the situation with the person I am angry at.

☐ Crying is a way I get my anger out.

☐ Journaling helps me think about my anger and gain more understanding.

☐ Sometimes I really need to hit something, so I use a punching bag.

☐ I draw my feelings.

☐ I talk with a friend about my feelings.

☐ I reach out to an adult I trust.

☐ I think positive things about myself.

☐ I go for a run or get some exercise.

☐ I take a bath or shower.

☐ I watch a funny movie or show.

☐ I read.

☐ I play a video game.

☐ I meditate.

☐ I engage in deep breathing.

☐ I think about thoughts or memories that make me happy.

☐ I go to my happy place, a place where I can imagine feeling calm.

☐ I listen to music.

☐ I think about the role I might have played in the situation.

☐ If I express my anger in a hurtful way, I figure out what to do differently in the future.

☐ I apologize if I hurt someone.

☐ I go outside and get some fresh air.

☐ I take a nap.

☐ I sing or dance.

☐ I play my favorite sport.

☐ _____

☐ _____

☐ _____

Write down the number of checked items.

Total: _____

The more boxes you have checked in the healthy category, the more helpful ways you know and use to manage your anger. Look over this list again. Are there any new ideas for managing anger that you think might work for you?

UNHEALTHY ANGER EXPRESSION

- ☐ When I am angry, I hate myself.
- ☐ When I am angry, I hate others.
- ☐ Breaking something helps me feel better.
- ☐ I often blame others for causing my anger.
- ☐ Screaming at people feels good when I am angry.
- ☐ I enjoy getting even with those who anger me.
- ☐ I cannot control my anger, ever.
- ☐ Anger is dangerous.
- ☐ I sometimes bully others to feel better.
- ☐ Anytime I am angry, I push it down and ignore it because I don't trust how I might react.
- ☐ Yelling terrible things about myself in the mirror helps me feel better.
- ☐ I think about hurting myself in some way to feel better.
- ☐ I pretend I am not angry and avoid thinking about it.
- ☐ If someone asks me what's wrong, I say "nothing."
- ☐ If someone asks me why I am angry, I scream at them.
- ☐ I hole myself up in my room and refuse to talk with anyone.
- ☐ I sometimes take a belonging of the person I am angry at and destroy it.
- ☐ I punch a hole in the wall.
- ☐ I believe anger is uncontrollable for everyone.
- ☐ I often refuse to apologize for my role in what happened.
- ☐ I sometimes write something mean about someone I am angry at on social media.
- ☐ I spread rumors about the person I am angry at.
- ☐ I use sarcasm when talking with the person I am having a conflict with.
- ☐ I throw or damage items around me, even my own.
- ☐ I feel powerless against my anger.
- ☐ I feel so overwhelmed when I am angry that it makes it hard to think.
- ☐ I sometimes don't remember what I did or said when I was angry.
- ☐ _____
- ☐ _____
- ☐ _____

Write down the number of checked items.

Total: _____

The more boxes you have checked in the unhealthy category, the more anger is probably impacting your life. The goal of this exercise is to help you better understand how much anger is managing your life so you can take control back.

In Real Life

TREVON was practicing playing the trumpet. He had a band competition over the weekend and wanted to make sure he was prepared. Recently, he had been told by different adults in his life that he had a poor attitude. This was really starting to get to him. He was getting all Cs (which was considered passing), had a part-time job, was in band, and babysat his siblings whenever his parents needed him to. Yet it felt like nothing he did was ever good enough. He often had trouble sleeping at night because his angry feelings would keep him awake. *Why do people expect me to perfect?* he thought.

Michelle was a straight-A student. She adhered to every rule at school and the rules her parents set. She always respected her parents and teachers, even when she did not agree with them. Lately, however, she'd started skipping her history class. She felt like her teacher was picking on her and it made her so angry. *This is literally the only thing I do wrong,* she thought. *I just can't bear that class. The pressure is too much.*

In Real Life

ALEX was flunking school. They didn't understand why it was important. They didn't want to go to school and had plans to work at their uncle's car shop. They liked cars and fixing them. Weren't you supposed to do what you like in life as opposed to what the world wants you to? *My friends are all about college and seem to have the impression that I'll be a complete failure in life if I don't attend with them*, thought Alex. Even though Alex had saved money from working to move out when they graduated high school and had a job lined up, their plan didn't feel good enough for people. Alex would become so angry that they would just retreat to their room to avoid dealing with it. Alex was recently starting to feel really bad about themself, care even less about school, and avoid their friends.

SONDRA was sick of everything. *Life is SO unfair*, she thought. *I don't have the things other kids had, my father is so strict since my mother left, and I'm not allowed to do anything fun. It's like he thinks I'll leave, too.* She had to watch her young siblings while her father worked. Her siblings were so poorly behaved that she had to raise her voice until they listened. Her father told her she shouldn't get so angry and that he just wanted what's best for her.

ANGER MANAGEMENT AT SCHOOL AND IN LIFE

There are many reasons you might be angry. You have pressures at school and/or home plus an endless number of rules being imposed on you everywhere you go. Your brain and body are developing and changing, and you are gearing up to make the huge shift of becoming an adult and living your own life.

With all this pressure come different responsibilities, such as doing more chores, getting a part-time job, learning to drive a car, and needing to develop life skills to live more independently.

School is probably where you spend most of your time, which has benefits but also many stressors. Homework adds up, and you're expected to complete it on a schedule imposed on you with no input while juggling all the other aspects of life.

To add to all this, social pressure can be really intense during the teen years. Friendships are such an important part of teen life. However, they can come with a lot of stress. Your friends may be struggling with their own different things, and they may not be there for you as much as you need them to be. You may have started developing romantic feelings for other people, which can feel great but can also include drama and moments of deep pain. Feelings of rejection from friends or romantic relationships can lead to feelings of sadness and anger like never before.

Unmanaged anger can impact your health in many ways. On top of this, anger can also negatively impact friendships, romantic relationships, and family relationships. Additionally, anger can interfere with focus and concentration, meaning you might have a harder time in school or even difficulty enjoying fun extracurricular activities such as sports, theater, or playing an instrument.

Anger that is allowed to become too powerful and out of control hurts one person the most: *you*. And you are the most important thing there is in your life!

The good news is that there are many things you can do to stop anger from being a problem in your life. In addition to learning ways to manage your anger in the moment, understanding the different day-to-day things that trigger your anger will allow you to discover techniques that will help you.

When you change your relationship with anger and how you express it, you will most likely feel a variety of shifts happening. You might begin to feel more confident, which means you will feel better about yourself and probably more motivated in your life. Your relationships will likely improve, meaning you will get along better with people in your life, including family and friends. Lastly, there is a good chance that you will see positive shifts in school, such as better grades and an increased ability to learn.

HOW TO COPE

There are many ways for us to express our anger. Some ways that might seem helpful are actually hurtful. One common expression that is actually not helpful is pretending we are not angry. We might do this in a variety of ways, like pretending it's not there, "locking it in a box" inside us, or doing something else anytime it comes up.

Another common reaction, which is the opposite of pretending it's not there, is to destroy objects or yell and scream at people. We might even get into physical fights or begin to do things that create serious trouble, which comes with a whole other series of intense consequences.

Neither of these ways of dealing is very helpful. Hiding our anger doesn't get rid of it. Often when we avoid the anger, it'll come out in ways we don't expect or plan for that are hurtful. When we do get it out physically, through yelling or fighting, we usually just feel bad about ourselves afterward.

What is helpful is this: When you notice that anger is happening, try to explore what is causing or fueling it, and then do something to address the cause. For example, you might get angry because your little brother broke your video game controller. So what are you going to do? If you're really mad, hitting or getting anger out in a physical way that does not hurt anyone or anything (such as using a punching bag or screaming into a pillow) is not bad. This can be a good first step to get out the anger that is bubbling over in a less hurtful way before you do something you might regret. However, the main goal is to notice the anger BEFORE you get to the breaking point and do something then. (This workbook has many exercises to help with this.)

When it comes to avoiding anger, we can create a fear or phobia of it. This isn't good because then, when it happens, it feels completely out of control and unmanageable.

By learning to confront anger, we learn ways to express it in ways that help us. For example, if you had a friend who was disrespectful to you and you avoided your anger because you were afraid of conflict, talking with someone about what happened or doing an activity to explore it like journaling can be very helpful. If you tend to express anger in outward ways, such as angry confrontation, yelling, or throwing things, you might try to relax your body or do something physical to release the anger, like listening to music, taking a walk, exercising, or playing a sport. We'll explore these options more in the upcoming exercises.

Regardless of how you currently express anger, this book will help you learn new ways to control your anger and ultimately feel better about yourself.

When to Get Help

When you're working on this book, there may be stories or exercises that touch on personal topics and evoke strong feelings. If you need to take a break from the book or space out the exercises, that's okay. There is no right or wrong way to work through this book. Just be kind with yourself and try your best.

Something happening in your life might make you need to pause this workbook, and you might need more one-on-one support from an adult. This is *not* a bad thing. Sometimes we might be so angry that we may do something that physically hurts ourselves or causes us great risk. There might also be times when the thoughts in our head are so negative or intense that we need to talk with someone, like a family member, teacher, or another trusted adult.

If talking with a trusted adult doesn't help, know that there are different ways to get support. You might talk with your school counselor or a therapist, or you might choose to attend a group with other teens who also need support. Sometimes things might be so overwhelming and out of control that it's necessary to stay somewhere overnight or for several weeks, such as at a hospital or treatment center, to get more in-depth help. It's all okay. There is additional support out there for you if you need it, and it's there to help. By getting the help you need, you will heal from whatever issues are affecting you, learn strategies to move forward in helpful ways, and live a fantastic life, knowing you have what it takes to get through tough times.

UNDERSTANDING YOUR ANGER

The first step to managing anger is finding out where it is coming from. Anger can come from a variety of sources. You might be stressed due to school. Events from your past might still be upsetting you. Current events may be causing pain and distress. You might have learned unhelpful ways to manage anger from the media, your friends, your siblings, or people in your family. Certain challenges might feel outside your control and might more easily trigger feelings of anger, such as difficulty learning or someone treating you poorly. You may even feel bad about yourself and not think you deserve to feel better.

This book is going to help you by teaching you how to identify what is causing your anger and giving you a variety of strategies to manage it. Not every strategy will work for everyone. We are all uniquely different. Some strategies might feel uncomfortable or unfamiliar, but this doesn't mean they aren't working. When we are used to addressing our anger in one way, it may feel very strange or even silly to try to address it in another way.

Give this book and yourself a chance. Try these new strategies and find out which ones help you control your anger as opposed to your anger controlling you. *You'll need to try a strategy several times before knowing if it works.* When you do something new, you can't expect to know how to do it well or for it to work perfectly the first time. Whether it's playing a new instrument, exercising, or learning any new skill, you will need to slowly build up your skills. The more you practice, the more success you will find. Before you know it, all these different strategies for managing your anger will become second nature.

Consider Your Strengths

Our brains are wired to notice danger, which can cause us to notice and focus on negative things, such as consequences from our actions or negative feedback we have received. Regardless of anything that we have done that might be considered bad, there is ALWAYS something good about ourselves.

Focus on what is going well for you. What are your strengths? What are your positive core traits? Write three.

1. _____

2. _____

3. _____

Great. Now celebrate them! Nothing is too little. Life is hard, and it is SO easy to focus on what is not going well. Read those positive words again and try to notice a pleasant feeling in your body when you do so. Feel good about being you.

If we feel terrible about ourselves, it is much harder to make the positive shifts we need to make in our lives. If we only focus on our mistakes, we forget about all the positives, and it will be harder to make consistent and lasting changes.

We don't need to feel bad about ourselves to change. We will actually change more easily and quickly if we are feeling good about ourselves from the beginning. We are human, and we all make mistakes; it can help to think some positive things about ourselves each and every day.

YOU CAN FEEL BETTER

Feelings come and go. It is perfectly normal to feel angry, stressed, overwhelmed, unmotivated, anxious—the list goes on. We don't usually initiate the feelings we are feeling ourselves; however, once they are there, it's our job to express them in a helpful way. We are not responsible for anger beginning, but to help ourselves, we need to try to figure out what it's related to and what it's telling us and then engage in an action to resolve it.

You may not realize that if you sit with your anger and try to do something to relax yourself or otherwise cope, the anger will pass, like an ocean wave or the wind blowing.

If you feel controlled by and powerless to your anger, know that this can change—you can learn to feel in control and know how to express anger in a positive way.

If you feel like anger is scary and so you avoid feeling it, you can shift to being able to feel your anger and express it in healthy ways.

The skills in this book will help you be more present and focused in the moment, identify more quickly the emotions in your body, and become a team with your feelings as opposed to being in combat with them.

For all of this, it's okay to take your time. Anger doesn't have an on/off switch. Instead, we are able to maintain changes by doing them consistently and slowly so they become a habit. Take it one moment at a time, and remember, you can do it!

LET'S GET STARTED

Maybe you've learned that some of the ways you are expressing your anger are not really helping you and that you need to make a change.

It might be hard, and it might feel uncomfortable.

These are both short-term emotions and experiences that will occur. However, we're playing the long game here. It's chess, not checkers. Short-term discomfort is going to pay off long term in many ways—the payoff is that you will continue your teen years or launch into adulthood in the best way possible to be a capable, strong, and healthy you.

Let's get started helping you make the positive changes you want in your life around managing anger.

YOU'VE GOT THIS.

PART TWO

EXERCISES TO UNDERSTAND YOUR EMOTIONS, MANAGE YOUR MOOD, AND BUILD COPING SKILLS

In part 2, we'll explore a variety of exercises that will help you identify why you are becoming angry, feelings that might be lurking underneath anger, the ways you think about things that might impact your anger, and strategies to help you shift from being controlled *by* your anger to being *in* control of your anger.

Let's get started!

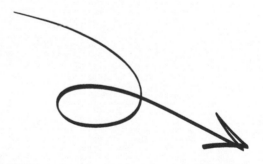

STRENGTH INVENTORY

Okay, so, anger is a problem in your life. This does not make you a bad person. We all get angry sometimes. And if we feel terrible about ourselves or believe that we are bad, it will be harder to learn new skills and use them consistently. It's easier to come at anger management from a positive attitude—like *I can do this!*

To get your head in a positive place, check out the following list of different strengths you possess. Put a check mark next to the ones that you feel strongly you possess and a W (for "working on it") for those you are working toward. There are three blank spots for you to write any strengths you have that aren't already listed.

☐ Smart

☐ Social

☐ Loving

☐ Creative

☐ Curious

☐ Open-minded

☐ Brave

☐ Fair

☐ Grateful

☐ Kind

☐ Honest

☐ Forgiving

☐ Funny

☐ Hopeful

☐ Protective

☐ Team player

☐ Spiritual

☐ Someone who loves to learn

☐ Able to laugh at myself (or the world!)

☐ Leader

☐ Role model for siblings or friends

☐ Artistic

☐ Courageous

☐ _____

☐ _____

☐ _____

Come back to this list throughout your work on this book or anytime you are feeling down on yourself. You're a wonderful person and deserve to feel good about yourself regardless of your past or any current behaviors. Some people even like to write down some of their strengths on sticky notes and post them in their room. Do whatever feels comfortable for you. As time goes on, you'll probably discover that some of those things you've been working on are now strengths!

ANGER TIME MACHINE

Sometimes we get so used to feeling anger, it can be hard to imagine living without it. Let's help you see how your life might look different without anger. This will help you realize ways that anger is impacting your life and give you an idea of some possible shifts.

This is called the "miracle question," and it goes like this:

If you woke up tomorrow and anger was no longer a problem for you, what would be different?

Answer the following prompts so you can see what this would look like for yourself.

ANGER TIME MACHINE

Three things that would be different:

_____

_____

_____

How would the morning go?

_____

_____

What would your friendships be like?

_____

_____

How would your interactions with your family look?

_____

_____

What would your free time look like?

_____

_____

CONTINUED

How would dinnertime go?

_____

_____

How would you feel about yourself?

_____

_____

How did this exercise go for you? I hope it helped you see the positive shifts that will occur when you take back control of your anger. Maybe it even gave you an idea of the specific parts of your anger that you might want to change—changes that have the potential to make all your tomorrows more promising!

STRESS CHECKLIST

Have you ever found yourself suddenly crying, feeling sad, or becoming angry for "no reason at all"? Most likely, our little friend *stress* was behind your feelings. Stress causes different chemicals to be released in your body (such as cortisol), which can increase your heart rate and cause muscle tension in your body. If you experience any mental health challenges, there is a good chance that stress will make it more intense.

You might be surprised that positive changes can lead to the same amount of stress as negative changes, which is why people often don't realize that stress might be behind whatever is going on for them. Seemingly fun things like going to parties, making new friends, and trying out different hobbies can cause big stress, too.

Following is a stress inventory. Put a check mark next to each item that you have experienced in the past six months, and let's see how much stress might be impacting your emotions, including your anger.

MY STRESS CHECKLIST

- ☐ Parental divorce/separation
- ☐ Breakup with a partner
- ☐ Breakup with a friend
- ☐ Starting a new relationship
- ☐ Death of a pet
- ☐ Death of someone you know
- ☐ A parent remarrying
- ☐ Poor grades
- ☐ Personal illness or injury
- ☐ A new sibling
- ☐ A change in schools
- ☐ Moving to a new house or a new city

- ☐ A change in teacher
- ☐ Learning challenges
- ☐ Mental health challenges in yourself
- ☐ Mental health challenges in someone living in your house
- ☐ Tension at home
- ☐ Tension at school
- ☐ Overcommitment and not enough downtime
- ☐ Tournaments/competitions
- ☐ Exams
- ☐ Vacation
- ☐ A birthday

The more items you checked, the more of an impact stress might be having in your life—but even one or two of these items can cause a lot of stress. Not to fear, though; the exercises in this book will also help you manage stress.

EMOTIONS TRACKER

To find out more about your emotions, tracking them can be super helpful. Following is a chart that I encourage you to use for a week. As you go through your week, focus on anger, but also track any other intense emotions you might experience. You can add more than one per day—just keep track of the time of day so you can spot any patterns.

DAY AND TIME OF DAY (MORNING, AFTERNOON, OR EVENING)	FEELING/ EMOTION	WHAT HAPPENED?	HOW DID IT MAKE ME FEEL OR ACT?	WHAT COULD HAVE BEEN DONE DIFFERENTLY?
Example: Sunday morning	Anger	Came home past curfew; got grounded	Yelled at my family member for ruling my life	I could have apologized and called to say I'd be late.
Monday Time of day:				
Tuesday Time of day:				
Wednesday Time of day:				
Thursday Time of day:				
Friday Time of day:				
Saturday Time of day:				
Sunday Time of day:				

What do you notice? Are there any patterns or recurring issues? Anything that worked well? What are three things that stand out for you when you look at the completed chart?

_____

_____

_____

_____

_____

_____

_____

_____

_____

_____

_____

_____

_____

_____

_____

_____

_____

_____

_____

_____

_____

ANGER TRIGGERS

It's really hard to work on your anger if you don't know what's making you angry. Anger triggers can be events that happen, thoughts we have about ourselves, interactions with people, or something else entirely. Following are some ideas of what anger triggers might look like.

Put a check mark next to each trigger that you have experienced. If you can think of others, feel free to write them on the blank lines. Then in the space that follows, write your top five anger triggers—the ones that happen to you most often. Look back over the Emotions Tracker that you created in the previous activity (page 20), as it probably identifies some of your triggers.

Once you know what's feeding the fire of your anger, you can begin to take action to resolve it and take control back from anger.

☐ Being told "no"

☐ Getting a bad grade

☐ Siblings annoying you

☐ Parents fighting

☐ Feeling criticized

☐ Feeling disrespected

☐ Not being able to do something

☐ Feeling like there is not enough time to complete what is expected

☐ Feeling as if the adults in your life have extremely high expectations of you

☐ Feeling as if no one really cares about you

☐ Someone being rude, mean, or disrespectful

☐ Feeling rejected by a friend or romantic partner

☐ Feeling pressured

☐ Being told rules you don't agree with

☐ Feeling taken advantage of

☐ Getting a consequence

☐ Unfairness

☐ Being jealous

☐ Not being left alone when you need space

☐ Being teased or bullied

☐ Feeling powerless

☐ Feeling rejected by another person

☐ _____

☐ _____

☐ _____

What are your top five anger triggers?

1. _____
2. _____
3. _____
4. _____
5. _____

Reflections: Thinking about this exercise, I realize . . .

_____
_____
_____
_____
_____
_____
_____
_____
_____
_____
_____
_____
_____
_____
_____
_____
_____
_____

THE UGLY SIDE OF ANGER

Everyone expresses anger in their own ways. Some of these are healthy, and some are, well, less healthy. Here is a list of some unhealthy ways—they often cause negative consequences for ourselves and others.

I scream at others.

I break objects (like my phone or tablet).

I punch walls or other objects.

I get into physical fights.

I throw objects.

I make hurtful or rude comments.

I seek revenge.

I roll my eyes so they can see me.

I pretend to hit someone.

I look physically aggressive.

I am passive-aggressive (meaning I indirectly express my emotions).

I lie.

I storm out.

I slam doors.

I purposefully push other people's buttons.

I gossip or spread rumors.

I harass a pet or other animal.

I ignore people or pretend like I cannot hear them.

Write down five scenes from a movie, book, television show, or even real life in which someone expressed anger in an unhealthy way and explain why it was unhealthy. Then write down how the person could have expressed their anger in a different way.

I'll go first. Let's take for an example our favorite boy wizard, Harry Potter. There is a scene in which Harry is hiding under an invisibility cloak and then throws mud at another wizard when that wizard says something insulting to his friend. Although this might have created a laugh, in the end, Harry was expressing his anger at the other boy in an unhealthy way. Was the other boy repeatedly mean? Sure. However, in the end, it is our responsibility, and a helpful skill for life, to express our anger in a healthy way versus a hurtful way.

List five ways someone expressed anger in an unhealthy way and why it was unhealthy.

1. _____
2. _____
3. _____
4. _____
5. _____

List five ways they could have expressed their anger in a healthier way and why it would be healthier.

1. _____

_____

2. _____

_____

3. _____

_____

4. _____

_____

5. _____

_____

ROOT CAUSES OF ANGER

You've thought critically about anger triggers from the Anger Triggers exercise (page 22). Underneath a trigger, there is usually something more going on—a root cause. I like to think about root causes as being in three categories:

1. Thoughts

2. Expectations

3. Boundaries

Let's explore them.

THOUGHTS

The way we think about something changes how we feel. If we change our way of thinking about something, it will shift our feelings. For example, if you think your friend is ignoring you because they didn't say hi when you saw them in the hallway, you might feel upset and rejected. If you stop and consider that maybe they have something on their mind and didn't even process that they saw you, you would probably feel understanding or sympathetic. You will explore this more in I Think, Therefore I Feel (page 28) and Thinking Conundrums (page 29).

EXPECTATIONS

We often have an idea in our head about how we want something to go—this is an expectation. Expectations can help us feel safe and in control. However, when something unexpectedly changes, we may feel disappointed, anxious, scared, or angry. This can make us feel powerless, which can then begin to feed the fire of anger.

BOUNDARIES

Boundaries are rules or limits that we set for ourselves and for others we are in relationships with. When our boundaries are not respected, we can get frustrated and angry. When we use anger in hurtful ways, we are often disrespecting other people's or even our own boundaries.

Take the next five to 10 minutes to journal about these categories. Consider if thoughts, expectations, and/or boundaries tend to be the most important or common categories for you. Think about ways you expressed your anger recently that were related to thoughts, expectations, and/or boundaries.

I THINK, THEREFORE I FEEL

The way we think about something changes how we feel about it, so if we change the way we think about something, we will change how we feel.

Try this exercise:

1. Get into a comfortable sitting position.

2. Close your eyes and imagine you are sitting on a park bench and in front of you is an extremely large lemon.

3. Imagine you put on some blue anger-tinted goggles. You look up at the sky, and it's a more intense shade of blue. You look around you, and the trees are teal. You look at a seagull and it looks blue.

4. Now look at the giant imaginary lemon in front of you. What color is it?

Through the blue anger goggles, the lemon will appear green. But in reality, it's yellow. And it only appears greenish due to the blue-tinted anger goggles—the way you're looking at it.

This is what anger does. It "colors" your view of reality. By changing the way you think about something, you will be able to change how you feel.

Reflections: Can you think of a situation that was colored by anger?

_____

_____

_____

_____

_____

_____

_____

_____

_____

_____

_____

THINKING CONUNDRUMS

There are four thinking patterns that can fuel the fire of anger. They are:

1. All-or-nothing thinking

2. Jumping to conclusions

3. Catastrophizing

4. Overgeneralization

ALL-OR-NOTHING THINKING

You can also call this *extreme thinking*, meaning that someone is taking one particular viewpoint and is unable to see anything but an extreme. If you are thinking in an *all-or-nothing* way, you might use words like *always, never, should, the worst ever*, and so on—like *I never get what I want*. The more you use these words, the more you will feel more intense emotions, and the greater the chance that you will engage in hurtful behaviors.

JUMPING TO CONCLUSIONS

This is when we assume something is true without having all the information we need to fully understand a problem. This can come out in two ways. One is called mind reading, meaning that we are assuming what someone else is thinking, like *My teacher always thinks I'm lying*. The second is called fortune telling, meaning that we are assuming what will happen in the future. This might come out like *I just know I won't be allowed to go to the party*.

CATASTROPHIZING

Catastrophizing is when we think that something bad that happened to us will lead to something far worse happening in the future; for example, *If I don't do well on this exam, I'm never going to get into college*.

OVERGENERALIZATION

Overgeneralization is when one bad thing happens to us and we assume that it is going to happen every time. For example, *My friend didn't come to my first game; I'm sure they'll never show up for me this season*.

CONTINUED

What are three things that made you angry recently?

1. _____

2. _____

3. _____

Consider if one of these four thinking patterns might have been the culprit. Can you think of some times that one of these thinking conundrums happened to you? Is there a way you could have thought differently about things that could have changed your feelings?

_____

_____

_____

_____

_____

_____

_____

_____

_____

_____

_____

_____

_____

_____

_____

_____

_____

EXTREME THINKING

You learned about all-or-nothing thinking in Thinking Conundrums (page 29). We talked about how this is also called *extreme thinking*. When we think in extremes, we are more likely to feel worse about a situation.

For this exercise, practice how these statements really feel and then journal about the differences in extreme versus more neutral statements.

Say the following extreme statements out loud, and then say the more neutral ones. See if you can come up with some of your own.

EXTREME THINKING STATEMENT	MORE NEUTRAL STATEMENT
I **never** get what I want.	I sometimes don't get what I want.
No one **ever** listens to me.	At times people don't listen to me.
Life is **always** unfair.	Life is unfair sometimes.
Everything goes wrong for me.	At times, things go wrong for me.
My parents **never** understand me.	Every so often, my parents struggle to relate to my point of view.
Everyone is mean to me.	A few people are mean to me.

Reflections: What are the differences between the extreme and neutral statements? Write down some extreme thoughts you've had before. What are their neutral counterparts?

_____

_____

_____

_____

_____

UNMASK THE ANGER: HIDDEN FEELINGS UNDER ANGER

Anger often tricks us into thinking we are angry when in reality it's covering up another feeling. These hidden feelings can include shame, sadness/hurt, fear/anxiety, rejection, or jealousy. It's important to understand when these emotions are fueling the fire of anger—just knowing that there's something underneath the anger will help us better manage the anger. Plus, it might shift what type of coping skill we choose to use in that moment—I'll show you those skills in Level Up (page 36).

Read these vignettes, and share what secret emotions might be occurring. Let's do the first one together.

Alphie was doing fine. They had one amazing best friend, were excelling in all their classes, and were on track to become the valedictorian for graduation. They loved to do art; however, recently they hated everything they drew. They would often become so upset at their drawings that they would begin to sob and scream, tear up whatever they drew, and then trash their room. This then caused Alphie extra stress due to needing to clean their room and taking time away from studying or doing more art.

The Hidden Feelings Under the Anger: Alphie was putting a lot of pressure on themself. Perhaps they are anxious about being good enough to become valedictorian. They might also be anxious about the big life changes coming up related to graduation and going away to college where Alphie knows nobody.

Now you try.

Rashida wanted to control her anger. However, sometimes she just felt so overcome by it, and without thinking, she would do things that got her into a lot of trouble, such as screaming at her teachers and getting into fights when she thought other girls were looking down on her for the way she looked. She hated looking dumb and felt this way anytime someone gave her feedback or said something rude to her.

The Hidden Feelings Under the Anger:

_____

_____

Hashem moved to the United States in middle school and really liked it. The problem was that his parents were very protective about his safety and were always hesitant to let him do things that other teens got to do. Because of this, he felt like he didn't fit in and didn't have the chance to go out and make many friends. He would become so angry that he would scream and throw things, and now he had begun to lie and sneak out.

The Hidden Feelings Under the Anger:

_____

_____

How did this exercise go? Was it hard to notice what feeling might be lurking underneath anger? Think about the last time you were very angry. What feeling(s) do you think was/were underneath it?

_____

_____

_____

_____

_____

_____

_____

_____

_____

_____

_____

_____

_____

_____

_____

SELF-CARE BASICS

Fact: When we aren't caring for ourselves, we are more likely to become angry or experience more intense emotions. Let's look at why.

NUTRITION/FOOD

What and when we eat impacts our mood. If we don't eat when we're hungry, we might be more likely to be irritated, annoyed, and so on. You know the term *hangry*? It's a real thing. Many people feel better eating foods that are full of nutrients, like fruits, veggies, nuts, and seeds. Also, undereating and overeating can happen more easily when we are stressed, so keeping an eye on your nutrition can be helpful.

EXERCISE

Research shows that consistent exercise reduces the risk of medical problems throughout a person's life and helps people live longer. Plus, people who exercise regularly report feeling calmer and happier overall than people who do not. Not surprisingly, when we are calm and happy, there is a good chance we will handle anger in a helpful way as opposed to a destructive way.

SLEEP

Sleep is a way for your body to physically heal and for your brain to process events from your day. When sleep is disrupted, you are more likely to get sick, have an increase in mental health challenges, and be easily irritated. Try your best to get eight to 10 hours of sleep a night.

What self-care area(s) do you feel strong in? What things might you need to shift? In the chart on page 35, write three ways you can commit to self-care changes. Make them manageable—not too overwhelming or drastic—and try to do them consistently. You can pick from the list of ideas or create your own.

Self-Care Ideas

Increase vegetable intake.

Eat three meals a day.

Run three times a week.

Sleep eight hours a night.

Increase sleep time by 30 minutes.

Walk five times a week.

Eat nutritious snacks.

Eat no more than one sugary snack a day.

Decrease soda drinking.

Turn phone and screens off an hour before bed.

SELF-CARE AREAS	SELF-CARE ACTIONS
	_____
Nutrition	_____
	_____
	_____
Exercise	_____
	_____
	_____
Sleep	_____
	_____

Reflections: Come back in a week—how did you do? Do you notice any changes?
Any improvements?

_____

_____

_____

_____

_____

_____

_____

_____

LEVEL UP

It can be useful to think about healthy anger coping skills as being in three categories. They are:

1. Distracting (avoidance)

2. Active (doing something in the moment when angry)

3. Preventive (taking actions to address potential future situations)

These skills are listed in order of ease. The simplest one to do is distracting, followed by active. Preventive is the most advanced.

To take the following self-quiz, choose each answer based upon how you might respond.

When I am angry about something that happens at home, I:
A. Watch YouTube.
B. Try to take several deep breaths.
C. Call a friend to talk out what happened so I can make a shift in the future.

When I am having a conflict with someone, I tend to:
A. Pretend I'm not angry.
B. Go for a run or exercise to release energy.
C. Try to have a conversation with the person to resolve what is happening.

I often have the urge to break things when I am angry, so I tend to:
A. Find something to take my mind off the anger.
B. Do something physical, like jump up and down, to get the anger out.
C. Journal about my anger to express my feelings and discover insights.

Some days I just wake up so angry, and then I:
A. Lie in bed and spend hours on social media or a game on my phone.
B. Think about what's making me angry and try to solve it.
C. Make sure I'm getting enough sleep, food, and exercise.

When a coach or teacher gives me feedback that angers me, I:
A. Try to think about something else.
B. Pause and count to 10 before speaking.
C. Consider what they are saying and then talk with another adult to get their thoughts.

Any coping skills are good skills, but having a balance of the different skills can make you best able to address anger in a variety of situations. We'll learn how in the next exercise.

If you answered mostly As, you lean toward distracting.

If you answered mostly Bs, you lean toward active.

If you answered mostly Cs, you lean toward preventive.

If you answered a mix, then you use all these coping skills.

Reflections: What did you learn about yourself in this quiz?

MENU OF COPING SKILLS

When we think about distracting, active, and preventive coping skills, I like to think of distracting like an appetizer, preventive like the main course, and active like the dessert. We want to have a little appetizer and a little dessert, but we are going to fill up on the main course.

Create your own anger menu by picking two from the distracting list, four from the preventive list, and two from the active list. Here are some ideas; you can also come up with your own.

DISTRACTING

→ Watch YouTube or other video platforms.

→ Spend time on social media.

→ Play video games.

→ Listen to music.

→ Avoid thinking about it.

PREVENTIVE

→ Talk with the person I tend to be angry at to figure out a different way to communicate.

→ Journal about my anger to try to notice insights.

→ Get enough sleep, food, and exercise.

→ Speak up when someone is pushing on a boundary I have.

→ Talk with my friends or an adult about what is bothering me.

ACTIVE

→ Take deep breaths to calm the body.

→ Go for a run or otherwise exercise.

→ Think about what is making me angry and try to solve it.

→ Jump up and down to get the anger out.

→ Count to 10 before responding or doing something.

Main Course (Preventive)

_____

_____

_____

_____

Appetizer (Distracting)   *Dessert (Active)*

_____   _____

_____   _____

_____   _____

_____   _____

Reflections: What do you think the barriers might be to using your menu? Is there anything you can do to combat them?

_____

_____

_____

_____

_____

DISTRACTION IS ACTION

Sometimes people feel completely overwhelmed by anger and have no hope that anything will work. Though distracting is a simple and basic coping mechanism, it's very valuable. Just doing something—anything else—can help us in the moment to make a healthier decision if our anger fire is raging. If that something can be something fun or silly, that can really help shift us away from the intense emotions of anger. Once you've conquered distracting skills, you can build on them and learn preventive skills. Here's a collection of ideas for distracting—feel free to add your own in the blank spaces.

Watch a movie or television show.	Take a walk.
Watch YouTube.	Count to 100.
Listen to music.	Jump up and down.
Make up a dance.	Name your favorite superheroes (or other characters).
Read a book.	Take a nap.
Play a video game.	Blow bubbles.
Cuddle a pet.	Eat.
_____	_____
_____	_____
_____	_____

Reflections: Which of these are you most likely to try?

_____

_____

_____

_____

_____

DEEP BREATHING

We have two nervous systems: the *sympathetic nervous system* and the *parasympathetic nervous system*. When we are calm and relaxed, our parasympathetic nervous system is online and in charge. But when we become activated—that is, when we feel an intense negative emotion—our sympathetic nervous system kicks in, and our prefrontal cortex (the part of the brain that helps with planning, learning, and following through) goes offline. When this happens, we have a hard time completing any of those skills that can help manage our anger.

What to do? Well, one of the easiest and quickest ways to shift back to our parasympathetic nervous system is to take five deep breaths. It's true. Easy peasy.

This exercise lets you try both fast and slow breathing so you can get a feel for the difference and how it works.

FAST BREATHING

1. Set a timer for 30 seconds.

2. Once you start the timer, breathe in and out as fast as you can comfortably until the timer goes off. This might sound a lot like a dog panting and might feel silly.

How does your body feel? I am going to guess that your heart is beating fast and your belly might be a little tired.

SLOW BREATHING

Now try breathing in and out slowly. There are a few ways to do this.

1. Take a deep breath in as you count to five, and then blow it out slowly as you count to five.

2. Now, hold your hands together, and when you breathe in, spread your hands apart like you are blowing up a balloon. When it's full, slowly breathe out, pushing the imaginary balloon back flat again.

3. Repeat either step 1 or step 2—whichever you liked better. Do at least five full, slow breaths, back to back.

How does your body feel? Most likely your heart is beating regularly now, and different parts of your body (like your heart, stomach, arms, and legs) might be feeling pretty relaxed.

The next time you start to feel anger in your body, take five deep breaths before you decide what to do with your anger. Take as many slow breaths as you'd like, but make sure five is the minimum.

ANGER VISUALIZATIONS

The mind is a very powerful thing. We can use our imagination to help us dream and create, but did you know we can also use our imagination to move through our anger? We have 100 percent control over our minds, and no one can take that away from us. We can even think things that are not real, and those thoughts cannot do any harm.

We don't want this skill to be the only way to manage our anger. But if we're stuck between doing something we might really regret and imagining doing it, then it's imagination for the win.

Ideas of things you can imagine are:

→ Dealing with the situation as if it were a video game

→ Crushing whatever is upsetting you

→ Aliens abducting whatever is angering you

→ Saying things that you want to say out loud in your head instead

→ Turning what is angering you into something silly

What are some other ideas you might be able to use next time?

_____

_____

_____

_____

Next time you're feeling angry, go ahead and draw your own imaginary scenario here.

MINDLESS MINDFULNESS

Calming our mind can be very helpful when we are angry. Once our mind is calm, our body will begin to relax. Try these mindfulness exercises when you are feeling calm, and see which one works the best. If you practice them first when you're calm, you'll be able to do them more effectively when you're feeling angry.

COUNTING

Count to 100. Count backward from 100. Count by 5s, 10s, or multiples of anything you like.

TAPPING

Tap your fingers all at once on a surface by you, whether it's a table, a notebook, or your own legs. Then start to make patterns. Tap every finger once. Tap every other finger once. Make up your own pattern.

DRAWING

Make random designs on a piece of paper with a pen, pencil, or colored pencil. You might draw in a circle and make concentric circles or scribble. You can even draw until there is no blank space left on the paper. Whatever works for you.

The goal of each of these exercises is to stop thinking about what is actually bothering you and help calm your brain and body.

Reflections: Trying these exercises, I realize . . .

PULL AND RELEASE

This is one of the best activities to do when you are really angry in the moment. To try it right now, all you need is a bath towel (or similar object) and a chair. Then follow the instructions. You can check out a link to a video tutorial in Resources for Teens (page 114).

1. Get a bath towel and twirl it up.

2. Place the towel on the ground in front of a chair.

3. Sit down in the chair and put both of your feet on the middle of the towel. Grab each end of the towel with your hands.

4. Pull the towel up with your hands and arms as hard as you can as you push down with your feet and legs just as hard.

As you do this, think of the thing you're angry about, and notice where you are feeling the anger in your body. Try to notice specifically where the anger is in your body. Keep pulling until you feel some relief from the anger or until your legs and arms are tired.

Reflections: Trying this exercise, I realize . . .

_____

_____

_____

_____

_____

_____

_____

_____

_____

_____

_____

_____

_____

_____

RELEASING ANGER ANYWHERE

When you feel so angry that you need to do something physical but you can't go outside, try these activities. You can check out a link to a video tutorial for all these activities in Resources for Teens (page 114).

PALM CRUSH

Take the palms of your hands and place them together, like you are clapping. Then push them together as hard as you can. Now push even harder. Most likely your arms will begin to shake. Do this for long as you need when angry. You can even imagine crushing whatever is making you angry.

WALL PUSH

Go to a wall that doesn't have anything on it. Press your hands against it and anchor your feet into the ground farther back. (You will be making an angle like a triangle when you do this.) Now, focus all your anger on the wall and try to push it. Keep going as long as you can. Imagine that you are releasing the anger from your body.

WALL SIT

Stand with your back to the wall and your feet a foot from the wall and shoulder-width apart. Slowly slide your back down the wall until you are "sitting" at a 90-degree angle. Hold this position for as long as you can. As you do it, focus on the anger you're feeling in your body and try to release it.

Try these exercises now, when you are not angry. Then, when you are angry, try them again and see which one works best for you. You might find that different ones work at different times.

Reflections: Trying these exercises, I discovered . . .

CONTAIN IT

The challenge with emotions is that they can come up at times when we don't have the space to process or explore them. A lot of people then push them to the side and try to never think about them again. You've learned that pushing emotions to the side, also called distraction or avoidance, can be helpful when the emotion is intense in the moment. But at some point, it's important to address what is happening. To start this process, it can be helpful to create an imaginary container.

The container can be anything—a Mason jar, shoebox, earbud case, and so on. Be as creative as you want.

Now, visualize putting whatever is upsetting you into the container. This is a new skill, so what you put in might come out. If this happens, kindly ask it to go back in, and visualize it moving back into the container.

At some point, take some time to think about whatever is in the container and figure out what you can do about it. You could do this while journaling, talking out loud, talking with a friend, or just thinking.

Take a few moments to journal about what might need to go into your container and if there is anything you can do to resolve it.

You can also draw your visualization here.

TARGET TOSS

When we are angry, we often feel bad about ourselves. In that moment, it can be helpful to do a task successfully to boost our confidence.

Target toss is a task that most everyone can accomplish, because you can create varying levels of difficulty. This activity can be as simple as crumpling a piece of paper and tossing it in a trash can. This simple technique can be a great way to focus on something that is not our anger and make us feel accomplished.

Here are a few other methods of target toss. Read through them and pick one or two that you can do.

1. Bounce a ball into a cup and then increase the difficulty by moving the cup farther and farther away from you.

2. Hit a target outside with a ball with your dominant hand. Increase the difficulty by throwing the ball with your nondominant hand, then over your shoulder, and so on.

3. Toss a balloon in the air and see how many times you can hit it without it hitting the ground.

4. Shoot a rubber band from your index finger at a target (like a trash can or a mark on a wall) and increase the difficulty as you are more successful.

5. Make a paper airplane and see how far you can launch it.

As you do these activities, visualize your anger hitting the target or basket.

IN CALM, OUT ANGER

Simply noticing what is happening in our body and then having an intention to shift it can be helpful. Following is a visualization exercise that can be helpful with anger, especially if you are feeling it stuck in your body. You can actually use this exercise for any feeling, such as sadness or anxiety.

1. Sit down in a comfortable position.

2. Notice where your anger sits in your body (such as your face, heart, stomach, or hands).

3. Imagine the anger is a color, such as red. Now imagine the anger breaking into tiny little dots of this color. Slowly blow the tiny dots out.

4. As you breathe in, inhale a color of dots that you enjoy, along with a calming feeling.

5. Keep doing this until as much of the new color is in and the red is out.

Reflections: How was this exercise for you? Do you feel more relaxed? Was it easy or hard? If it was hard, what was hard about it? Journal about these questions or any other thoughts you have about the exercise.

CREATIVELY ANGRY

When we are angry in the moment, focusing on it actively can help us move through the anger and even gain some insight into what's happening.

Here are some different creative categories and specific ideas to help you move through anger.

DRAWING

Draw a picture of what your anger looks like.

Draw a picture of what's making you angry.

Draw a fantasy resolution and then a real one.

CLAY

Create your anger.

Create what is making you angry and then destroy it.

Create something random.

BUILD

Build a card tower and then knock it down.

Build a LEGO or block figure that represents your anger.

Make a figure of what is making you angry and then break it apart.

VIDEO GAMING

Create a world in a video game where you can go when angry to feel better.

Create a world where you can put your anger so it can take a vacation.

SONGWRITING

Write a song about your feelings.

Write a rap about your feelings.

Write a poem about your feelings.

How about testing out one of the ideas here?

GIVING ANGER THE MIC

By talking about what is bothering us or simply saying out loud what is going on, we can start to figure out the situation, think through it, and get it out of our brain and body. When we hold on to something, it can often make it more intense. When we talk about it, we relieve some of the pressure that is building up. When this happens, anger is less likely to explode and come out in hurtful ways.

Journal about your anger using these prompts.

When I am angry, I wish:

_____

_____

The positive side of my anger is:

_____

_____

The worst part of my anger is:

_____

_____

If I were less angry, I would be:

_____

_____

I learned my anger from:

_____

_____

I wish my anger knew:

_____

_____

A CHILL PLACE

Another way to regulate your anger is to create a place you can go to in your brain to help calm your body. Think about a place you would like to go. It doesn't have to be real and can be made up of different places you love. Let your imagination soar. As you think about the place, focus on noticing what is happening with all five senses.

For example, my calm place is a lagoon in the middle of a forest.

I see: Trees, blue water, flowers, animals. The sky is dark with bright lights from the aurora borealis.

I hear: The sound of water on the shore. Birds chirping. My favorite song.

I smell: Flowers, lavender, coffee, chocolate, and rain.

I taste: Vanilla.

I feel (physical and emotional): The ground holding me secure as I lie on the grass. A warm calmness in my body. The grass under my feet.

Now you try it.

I see:

_____

_____

_____

_____

I hear:

_____

_____

_____

_____

CONTINUED ⟶

I smell:

_____

_____

_____

_____

I taste:

_____

_____

_____

_____

I feel (physical and emotional):

_____

_____

_____

_____

ANGER CALENDAR

Okay, so, this may seem weird. But schedule a time to connect with any anger you may be feeling. And not only feel it, but also say out loud anything that makes you angry, frustrated, annoyed, or any other emotion. And as you do so, jump up and down, walk around, and MOVE your body. Often we become angry because things we don't realize are bothering us are beginning to build up, and then we boil over. If we make space to just let our feelings out, it will help us recognize that something is wrong and will also allow us to begin to express it, which will keep it from building up AND release it before it's overwhelming.

Take a few moments and practice doing this right now. Then look at your schedule and put a reminder on your calendar or set an alarm for a day and time every week when you can do this. Use the chart below to fill in how your first few days with anger went.

	DAY 1	DAY 2	DAY 3
I was angry about:			
How I moved/ what I said:			
How I felt afterward:			

CONTINUED ⟶

Reflections: How was that for you? What do you feel you learned? What was the most helpful part?

_____

_____

_____

_____

_____

_____

_____

_____

_____

_____

_____

_____

_____

_____

_____

_____

_____

_____

_____

_____

THE ILLUSION OF CONTROL

In life, there are some things we can control and a whole lot we can't. Anger often comes up when we can't control a situation and become frustrated. External control refers to all the things that we do not have control over, such as the amount of homework we get, a friend flaking on us, or being bullied. Internal control is what we CAN do in a situation, such as changing the way we think or react, engaging in a coping skill, or getting support from an adult.

Take a look at this example, then consider the internal and external factors underlying the situation.

Quintin is often sad, which then comes out as anger. He doesn't have many friends and is too shy to make them. He is at times bullied at school and doesn't stand up for himself because he is afraid. He then becomes easily angered at his parents and the few friends he does have. This has resulted in his best friend not wanting to spend that much time with him.

Internal: How he engages with his friends. Working on his shyness. The way he responds to bullies and getting adult support.

External: Being bullied. Friends holding their own boundaries and not spending as much time with him.

Now, think about a situation in your own life that may cause you to feel anger. What is it? Fill in the blanks to try to work out the internal and external aspects. The goal is to find out what you actually have control over versus what you do not.

Internal:

_____

_____

External:

_____

_____

Reflections: Thinking about this exercise, I realize . . .

_____

_____

_____

_____

AN INTERVIEW WITH ANGER

Have a conversation with your anger by letting it answer the following questions. Sometimes giving anger a voice can help build understanding around it.

QUESTIONS FOR ANGER

How are you?

_____

_____

_____

_____

What do you need?

_____

_____

_____

_____

How are you trying to help me?

_____

_____

_____

_____

Now talk to your anger. Explain where you are coming from:

A Conversation with Anger

Thank anger for helping you and share how it has done so.

_____

_____

_____

_____

Let anger know which new skills you have learned to help you feel better.

_____

_____

_____

_____

_____

Let anger know that you do not need its help as much anymore and invite it to take some time off.

_____

_____

_____

_____

_____

Visualize anger going on vacation and tell it that you will transport it back if you need its help.

_____

_____

_____

_____

_____

INNER CRITIC

Sometimes anger is fueled by our inner critics. Our inner critics say things that can be like a You-Tube video on a loop or our own negative playlist set on repeat. We often don't realize that these statements are going on in the background. Angry feelings might make these negative thoughts *seem* like the truth, but they are not.

Here are common statements an inner critic might make:

I am not good enough.

There is something wrong with me.

This is too hard for me to handle.

I cannot keep close friends.

They will always be smarter than me.

Now, try shifting your perspective. This is where you take a negative thought or situation and change it with alternative statements or thoughts.

For example, if you get an F on a test, here is a way to change your perspective and overcome your inner critic:

INNER CRITIC STATEMENTS	ALTERNATIVE POSITIVE THOUGHTS
I got a bad grade, so I am dumb.	1. I made a mistake and didn't study as much as I could have.
	2. Grades don't define my worth..
	3. I learn more from mistakes than from always succeeding.
	4. I am smart.
	5. I did the best I could.

The next time you are angry, notice what exactly is happening and what your inner critic is saying. Once you notice what they are saying, you can replace the negative statements with more positive alternative ones.

In the chart, write any statements coming from your inner critic and come up with alternative positive thoughts.

INNER CRITIC STATEMENTS

ALTERNATIVE POSITIVE THOUGHTS

WALK AND NOTICE

Being outside is calming. For this exercise, go for a walk. As you walk, instead of thinking about your day or everything you need to accomplish, simply notice what is happening around you. Put your five senses (seeing, hearing, smelling, feeling, tasting) to work to see if you can notice three things from each sensory category.

Alternately, here is a list of things you might find. See how many things on this list you can find. Put a check mark next to every item you see outside. You can also come up with your own list.

- ☐ A purple car
- ☐ Bugs
- ☐ Pink flowers
- ☐ A tree with nuts or fruit on it
- ☐ A parent with a child
- ☐ A group of friends
- ☐ Gum on the ground
- ☐ A cat

- ☐ A basketball hoop
- ☐ A dirty car
- ☐ Something broken
- ☐ A bird
- ☐ A penny
- ☐ A puddle
- ☐ A cloud

As you learn to become more mindful, you'll notice more things around you. Try to do this as often as possible—several times a week if you can, especially if you feel worked up or had a bad day. If your thoughts drift, bring them back to the present moment. Try to notice something new each time. It will help you slow down your mind, be mindful, and feel more relaxed and ready for anything life might throw your way.

SUPPORT ENTOURAGE

When we are feeling down on ourselves, it can be hard to think about nice things or even to offer support to ourselves. If you can relate, here is a visualization that might be helpful for you.

Pick a place that's relaxing, calm, or exciting. It could be somewhere you have been or even the Chill Place you created earlier (page 53). Imagine yourself there, and focus on your five senses. Imagine you are surrounded by people who support and love you, like your parents and close friends—think about who they are. Now let's add in your favorite characters from TV, books, or movies. Be as creative as possible.

MY SUPPORT ENTOURAGE

Where are you, and what do you see? _____

_____

Who is there? _____

_____

What are they saying to you? _____

_____

How do you know they support you? _____

_____

How do you feel as a result? _____

This is a great exercise to use when you are feeling down on yourself (for example, if you expressed your anger in a hurtful way).

Your support team will still like and love you, even if you have trouble with liking or loving yourself. They'll tell you what you need to hear!

NOW VERSUS LATER

Making changes in yourself can be hard. Avoiding changes is much easier.

Avoiding has a big short-term payoff, meaning we get rewarded right away by not having to deal with the issue. But taking the time and energy to work on anger will pay off long-term. It can be really hard to want to work toward our future. But think about it: You're doing it all the time. Getting good grades helps you have options if you want to go to college, going to band or sports practice helps you get better, and practicing any skills helps in the long run.

Working on our anger is the same. Short-term, it may feel good to avoid it or express it in unhealthy ways. However, long-term, doing so can have bigger consequences.

Following are a few examples of situations in which teens need to decide the best long-term option that will cause fewer consequences and leave them feeling better about themselves. Read the scenarios and see if you can recognize the healthy option in each situation.

Scenario 1: Rebecca screamed at her parents often. They set up a positive reinforcement system, agreeing to buy her a pair of expensive shoes if she stopped screaming when angry.

Which of these would be a healthy long-term option for Rebecca?
A. Keep yelling at her parents because she knows it upsets them.
B. Work with her parents by trying to manage anger so she can get the new shoes.
C. Continue screaming and increase the behavior if she does not get the shoes. Her parents often give in anyway.

Scenario 2: Steven didn't like his teacher because he was getting bad grades in her class. He would often make rude comments under his breath during class because he was so angry at her.

Which of these would be a healthy long-term option for Steven?
A. Start saying the comments more loudly in case she didn't hear them in order to be more clear about his dislike for her.
B. Try to understand why he is so angry at her and consider his own role in what is happening.
C. Take a deep breath after he says each comment to try to calm down but keep making the comments.

Scenario 3: Sergey gets into fistfights with other teens. If someone disrespects him, they will get what they deserve.

Which of these would be a healthy long-term option for Sergey?

A. Begin to shove instead of punch. Because that's less intense, it's a better option to slowly help him shift away from the behavior.

B. Punch harder—then maybe the other teens will learn to leave him alone.

C. Consider if he's really being disrespected or if others are simply trying to annoy him because they know he has a short fuse. When someone disrespects him, he can consider leaving the situation and try to get his anger out in another way, such as by going for a run or practicing boxing.

HIDDEN COST OF ANGER

Although anger can make us feel like we have control, there is a secret cost to it. That cost is often trust. The more we express our anger in hurtful ways, the more likely we will lose the trust of the people in our lives and have to repair it. Write the names of three people who you might need to apologize to about your anger and what you might say. Even if you're not ready to say it to them yet (though I highly encourage you to do it), it will feel good to think about making peace, improving your relationship, and getting their trust back.

PERSON 1   Name _____

How trust may have been lost _____
_____
_____

What I would say to apologize _____
_____
_____

PERSON 2   Name _____

How trust may have been lost _____
_____
_____

What I would say to apologize _____
_____
_____

PERSON 3   Name _____

How trust may have been lost _____
_____
_____

What I would say to apologize _____
_____
_____

Reflections: Thinking about this exercise, I realize . . .

OVERCOMING SHAME AND APOLOGIZING

We are not our actions. Just because we might behave in hurtful ways does not mean we are terrible people. Shame can make someone feel like they are a bad person after they do something embarrassing instead of simply feeling like they made a fixable mistake. Shame does not motivate us; in fact, it usually makes us feel worse. When we feel terrible about ourselves, our feelings are hard to change.

In the previous exercise, you worked on recognizing what apologies you might need to make. Now it's time to forgive the most important person.

You.

Write down three memories you have of feeling embarrassed or shameful about the way you handled anger. Holding on to these memories and feeling bad about yourself takes a lot of energy and effort. By letting go of them and making a decision to do something different in the future, you can feel relieved and hopeful.

The goal is to learn from our mistakes as opposed to being held emotionally captive by them.

As you write down your three memories, think about what happened for you to react negatively because of your anger, consider what you will do in the future if you face a similar situation, and then let the memory go.

After you write these memories down, you can tear them into tiny pieces and flush them down the toilet, recycle them, bury them outside—do whatever YOU NEED to FORGIVE YOU.

Memory 1: _____

_____

Why did you react this way?

_____

What will you do differently in the future?

_____

Now let the memory go.

Memory 2: _____

_____

Why did you react this way?

_____

What will you do differently in the future?

_____

Now let the memory go.

Memory 3: _____

_____

Why did you react this way?

_____

What will you do differently in the future?

_____

Now let the memory go.

CONTROL OTHERS BY CONTROLLING YOU

This may sound strange, but sometimes you can actually control other people in your life—not in a supervillain-taking-over-the-world kind of way, of course, but more in a kind and respectful way. When people are kind, honest, open, and respectful, other people tend to want to help them or listen to them more. If there are people in your life to whom you are not always respectful or kind, changing this could lead to some positive results.

Think about your parents. How would they engage with you differently if anger was less of a problem in your life? How would your friends? Teachers? Peers? Romantic partner?

Here's one example of a dynamic that would change if there was more trust in the relationship.

Jezabell has received most everything she has wanted in life. Recently, though, she has started to argue more with her parents, mostly about them wanting her to check in with them every few hours when she is out with friends. Jezabell refuses. *It's my time with friends, and it has nothing to do with my parents. They wouldn't ask me to text every few hours if I was in my room doing home-work.* Her parents were being so controlling and had now begun taking things away. First it was her tablet, then her gaming console, and now her phone. She fumes, *How am I supposed to check in when I have no phone?*

What could Jezabell do differently? What might her parents do in return?

CONTINUED ⟶

What are some examples of people in your life that you could change your behavior around? A family member? Teacher? Friends?

Person 1: _____

What would you do differently? _____

_____

_____

_____

_____

Person 2: _____

What would you do differently? _____

_____

_____

_____

_____

What do you need to make a change? What is your plan moving forward?

_____

_____

_____

_____

_____

_____

_____

A DAY IN ANOTHER'S LIFE

Have you ever heard the advice "Try to put yourself in someone else's shoes"? It may sound simple, but it can be very powerful. Sometimes we can be so absorbed in our own world that we don't see that someone else's actions have absolutely nothing to do with us—even if they do affect us.

When we realize this, it can often remove the power from our anger and will actually help us have empathy and compassion. We are then more likely to realize that it's not about us.

This also works in reverse. Sometimes we might think we are mad at someone and direct our anger at them. However, it could be that we are actually angry about something else.

Use the prompts below to spend some time contemplating what else could be going on.

Is there someone in your life who directs their anger at or around you? Who is it?

_____

_____

What is going on in their life?

_____

_____

_____

Could the things they are doing that upset you really be about something else entirely?

_____

_____

Is there someone in your life you might be directing your own anger at?

_____

_____

Reflections: Thinking about this exercise, I realize . . .

_____

_____

_____

_____

_____

_____

CATCHING ANGER EARLY

I have had so many conversations with someone who, when I reflect that they might be angry about something, replies, "I'm not angry, I'm just annoyed," which is often another word for anger. Often these little annoyances begin to build up and can lead to anger explosions—a boiling point. If you begin to understand and then notice this buildup of annoyance or some other negative feeling, you'll be able to more effectively use the skills to manage your anger well before it boils over.

Look over some of the different words for anger that follow—they're listed in random order. You can use your own words if you like. Then choose the ones that describe the buildup of your anger. Start filling in the thermometer from the bottom up. Make the first five words what your anger feels like when it is just beginning, the middle five words what your anger feels like when it gets bigger, and the last five words for the most intense feelings of anger. By determining this scale, you'll be able to begin to use different coping skills as soon as you begin to feel the first clues of anger.

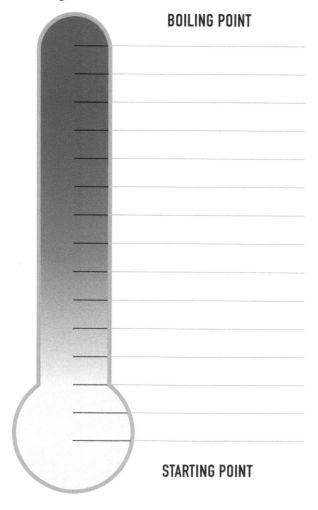

BOILING POINT

STARTING POINT

POSSIBLE FEELINGS
Grumpy
Annoyed
Frustrated
Peeved
Pissed
Rageful
Ballistic
Huffy
Smoldering
Fuming
Shocked
Uncomfortable
Explosive
Upset
Ticked off
Irritated
Outraged

LETTER TO YOUR PAST AND FUTURE SELVES

It's important to honor who you have been, who you are currently, and who you are becoming. You most likely have made some changes even while you have been reading this workbook, and you will surely make more changes as you continue to grow.

Write a letter to your past and future selves and pick a date in the future (maybe at the end of this workbook or in a few months) to review it. You can even write a new letter if you're still working on your anger when you read it. This can be a helpful way to honor where you have come from and what you are hoping for the future.

Dear past self,

I want you to know that: _____

_____

_____

_____

I forgive you for: _____

_____

_____

_____

I have learned: _____

_____

_____

_____

Thank you for: _____

_____

_____

_____

CONTINUED ⟶

Dear future self,

My hope for you is that: _____
_____
_____
_____

I will try to: _____
_____
_____
_____

I am excited for: _____
_____
_____
_____

I know you can: _____
_____
_____
_____

When things are hard, please remember: _____
_____
_____
_____

I look forward to: _____
_____
_____
_____

PERSONAL ANGER MANAGEMENT PLAN

You have learned a lot about anger. You've learned the different levels of coping skills: distracting, active, and preventive. You've learned what feelings might be hiding under your anger. You've discovered tools to manage anger in the moment and how to prevent anger from taking control.

Based on the exercises you've done, create a personal anger management plan—a cheat sheet of sorts. Having all these notes in one place will enable you to access them quickly and review them for when you might need them. Read this list daily or weekly to help your brain and body integrate them into your daily life.

My triggers (page 22):

_____

_____

Best distracting techniques to use in the moment (page 39):

_____

_____

Best active techniques to do in the moment to release (page 39):

_____

_____

Best preventive techniques to prevent anger from taking over (page 39):

_____

_____

My strengths (page 16):

_____

_____

Take Stock of Your Progress

Sometimes we lose track of how far we've come as we work toward our goals. Let's take a few minutes to go back over the healthy and unhealthy anger checklists from the beginning of the workbook (pages 4 and 5). Go through those lists again, and compare your new scores today to your original scores. How'd you do? What did you notice was different this time? Reflect here on some of the changes that have really made a difference for you.

_____

_____

_____

_____

_____

_____

_____

_____

_____

_____

_____

_____

_____

PART THREE

MANAGING ANGER IN REAL LIFE

Do you realize how much you've learned? You've stockpiled a bunch of skills to manage your anger. Now let's take a look at some real-life situations that other teens have experienced. In this section, teens will share their experiences and questions, and I'll respond to them with different tips, tricks, and advice on how to handle the situation in helpful ways. You can then apply these tips to your own life to more easily express and manage your anger.

Q+A 1

Q: My parents take my cell phone every night at 9 p.m. But nighttime is when all my friends are up and available to talk, so now I am being left out. It's starting to make me feel angry. What can I do to make my parents understand how this is affecting my life? Is there a way to convince them to let me use my phone?

A: Being a teen is so hard because parents often get to control the rules. In situations like these, it can be helpful to talk with your parents about what their concerns are. By hearing their perspective, it will help you build empathy and remove the power from your anger. You explored this earlier in the workbook in A Day in Another's Life (page 73). Once you have listened to their concerns, explain where you are coming from. Then, work together to see if there is a reasonable compromise. For example, you could ask them to consider the rules for the weekend. Or you could ask, "Is there a change you need to see in me in order to make this happen?" For example, if you often refuse to give your parents your phone, they are most likely not going to want to be flexible. But if we're willing to change a little, the other person is more likely to change a little as well.

Is there something the teen in this example could shift? Is there something in your personal life that could benefit from a shift?

Q+A 2

Q: My teachers give so much homework when they already know we are busy. My math teacher is the worst. He is always embarrassing me in front of the class. He knows math is hard for me and calls on me anyway. How can I deal with this?

A: Teachers hold a lot of power in a teen's world. It can be really frustrating when someone who is there to support you doesn't really do so. And it can feel even worse if it seems like they are purposely picking on you and causing you more pain. This can often cause you to feel embarrassed, which is the icing on the ick cake.

Something I have noticed is that many teens don't want to talk with their teachers. I understand that talking does not always work, and some teachers are truly challenging or hard to deal with and may not be receptive. However, in my experience, teachers usually want to hear from their students and are far more open to talking about what is happening than you might assume.

If you're having a hard time with a teacher and/or a class, tell an adult family member about your struggles. Talking it over with a trusted adult will help you figure out how to frame the conversation with your teacher. Then, schedule a time to talk with your teacher. This could be simply to ask for help or share your concerns. What's the worst that could happen? A positive benefit is more likely than the worst-case scenario.

If you are having trouble deciding what to do, a few questions to ask yourself are:

1. Am I avoiding something? _____

2. If so, is there a real fear? _____

3. What outcome am I hoping for from this meeting? _____

4. Do I need my parents to help support me in this? _____

Q+A 3

Q: I'm getting frustrated with my dad. He's great, but he sometimes breaks his word. He's supposed to pick me up every other weekend, and multiple times he has not come. Then he promises to take me somewhere special and doesn't. Then he will buy me a gift and pretend like nothing even happened. He says that keeping your word is important, yet he breaks his word and it seems hypocritical. How can I move past my anger and enjoy spending time with him again?

A: It's hard when adults expect something that they don't do themselves. This can make teens want to break rules and not spend time with them, and it can makes teens angry. Is there a way for you to share with your father what is happening? It's also important to consider whether he's going through something difficult in his life, which could make it hard for him to show up in the ways he wants to for you.

Earlier in the workbook, you learned how to discover other causes of anger in Unmask the Anger (page 32). You can use this same skill to explore what is going on for someone else. Try using it to identify what might be going on with your father. Using this skill takes the power away from anger, increases understanding of the other person, and often gives you empathy. I encourage you to try this with your father. Then talk it through with him.

Q+A 4

Q: One of my friends constantly leaves my messages on read and then gets mad at me when I call them out in person for ignoring me. Why do they react like this? I am just sticking up for myself.

A: Feeling ignored by friends can feel pretty hurtful. And sticking up for yourself is important, but calling someone out or criticizing them is not the healthy way to do this. Being able to have difficult conversations with your friends is an important skill. I use the word *skill* because it really is a skill, and it can be easy for someone to interpret it the wrong way if it's not done carefully. It's likely your friend reacts with anger because they felt harassed, even if that was not your intention.

Ask yourself the following questions before you stick up for yourself. Use this as an opportunity to reflect on yourself and consider the consequences of any actions.

1. What am I hoping to get out of this?

2. Am I expressing myself in a way that can be heard?

3. If it were me, how would I like someone to talk with me?

4. Is there another way to say this that might be nicer?

Another idea is to ask the friend who is mad at you if they could share specific reasons why they don't agree with the way you're sticking up for yourself. They might share information that helps you understand where they are coming from. Listen to them and stay calm throughout the conversation. By opening a discussion, hopefully you'll both be able to get your feelings out on the table and work through your problem.

Use the following lines to answer the preceding list of questions.

_____

_____

_____

_____

_____

_____

_____

Q+A 5

Q: I have a learning disability, and another kid keeps making fun of me. I try not to let it get to me, but deep down it makes me upset. I often don't care for myself in ways I should because of this angry feeling. Can I do anything to feel better?

A: It sounds like you may have turned your anger at being treated poorly by others into anger at yourself. When this happens, you might think badly about yourself, not take showers, eat poorly, begin to see friends less, and have dark thoughts. These actions can make you feel even worse.

First, please know that you deserve better. Someone else's mean words or actions do not define you. Next, I want you to know that you can take steps to make things better. Have you reached out to an adult to get support? I definitely recommend talking with a family member or another trusted adult and a counselor at school or outside school. They can help you work on building your self-esteem and address any bullying that may be happening.

To begin to deal with these feelings, try this exercise. It's called a bubble or shield exercise. Follow the instructions. You can also find a link to a video tutorial in Resources for Teens (page 114).

1. Get into a comfortable position and imagine that you have a clear bubble around you, protecting you from the outside world. Only you can allow something inside your bubble.

2. Similar to the Chill Place activity (page 53), add anything to your bubble that is soothing or relaxing to you.

3. When someone says something mean or hurtful, imagine the words approaching the outside of your bubble and then rolling or bouncing off it.

4. As you do this, think about positive things about yourself, including anything positive that could combat or battle the hurtful comments.

Q+A 6

Q: My grandparents are really strict. When they try to impose their rules, we sometimes get into screaming matches. I made some mistakes before with my anger, and now they question everything I do. This makes me so angry that I don't want to visit them anymore. What do you do when you have to be around someone who makes you so angry?

A: This sounds like it's very painful. It's hard to feel good about yourself when you are not getting positive validation. Adults really want to teach skills and values so that the children they love can live good lives. Could this be a reason your grandparents have so many rules?

Also, it sounds like trust was broken and has not been repaired. I wonder if you can try talking with your grandparents about this, including asking them what needs to shift for them to trust you more.

You don't have control over your grandparents' choice to yell at you. However, you do have control over your response and whether to yell back at him. Maybe you can come to an agreement to not yell at one another. Staying calm when talking is important for everyone involved. Maybe you can come up with a hand signal as a reminder to chill if a person raises their voice.

I also hear that you don't want to be around them—this is really hard, especially because it may be impossible to avoid them. Sometimes people give off nonverbal cues of communication—also called being passive-aggressive—which can aggravate the other person. People can do this to purposefully upset others and pretend like they are not actually doing anything wrong. Other times they might be doing it unconsciously, meaning they do not realize they are doing it.

I encourage you to think about what might be going on for you, what pieces you can shift, and if you could have a conversation with your grandparents about the pieces that only they can shift.

Q+A 7

Q: My sister can be really inconsiderate and she never leaves me alone. She knows that I don't like people touching my stuff, but she comes in my room and moves my stuff or takes items of mine, even when I have asked her not to. The other day I lost it and screamed at her. Now my parents took away all my screens, in their words, "until you can be respectful to your sister." What about *her* being respectful to *me*? I'm always being told I have to be nicer to her because I'm the oldest and she has a disability. How can I control my anger without taking it out on my sister and parents?

A: It's difficult when we feel that we have extra responsibility and that we are being treated unfairly. When someone is doing something that's not nice to us, I often encourage people to try to put themselves in that person's shoes, like in the exercise A Day in Another's Life (page 73). Sometimes our younger siblings look up to us and want our attention. Even negative attention is attention. I wonder if she wants to spend more time with you. You could directly ask her and see what she says. You could also just spend a little more time with her and see if something shifts.

It can be especially hard when a sibling has a disability. Try to remember that it is not something that she can change, nor does it mean something bad about her. What might be more helpful is to focus on her strengths and the ways in which you two do get along.

Also, when things are calm, you can make sure that your parents are aware of what is happening and explain to them what you're dealing with to help them understand how upsetting it is to you. Sometimes parents don't see what we see or realize that something is bothering us as much as it is.

Q+A 8

Q: When I am angry, the only thing that really helps is getting into a fight. It's causing a lot of problems for me, but I dont want to change. I don't know what else to do. How can I solve this?

A: Anger can help us feel powerful and in control in the moment. But really, the opposite is true. Anger is controlling us, and the problem with this is that as you get older, the consequences will become more severe, and your parents or guardian or a school won't be the only ones weighing in—it becomes a legal issue. Learning to control your anger now will help you avoid becoming an adult who expresses anger physically.

It sounds like when you are angry, releasing it physically is what your body needs. Sometimes this makes people feel bad about themselves, but my hope is that they do not. Remember in the beginning of the book when we talked about the brain and the nervous system (page 41)? You are the type of person who goes into fight mode when you are activated. If using a calming in-the-moment activity such as deep breathing (page 41) does not help, it means you need to do something physical first to help release the anger from your body.

You've gotten into the habit of releasing your angry energy by hitting or getting into physical fights. But there are many other ways to get your anger out that will not get you into trouble. For example, look back at the Menu of Coping Skills (page 38). Anything physical that does not get you into trouble will work. Do push-ups, jump up and down, run around in circles, do burpees, punch a punching bag, and so on. Do anything helpful that will help you settle your body down.

Q+A 9

Q: My family is really into sports, and it's just not something that interests me. I'd rather draw or play video games. I don't fit in with them. It makes me angry but I don't even care to do anything about it. How am I supposed to cope?

A: When we are emotionally hurt, we may try to control the situation by pretending that we don't care. But not doing anything is still doing something.

As you get older, the consequences of avoidance can have a big impact on your future relationships. Learning how to understand exactly why you're angry about what is going on in the moment and dealing with it will help you deal with conflicts in the future.

I recommend that you journal about why you feel like you don't fit in. This will help you gain insight into what's really going on inside you and be able to have a conversation with your parents. Are there old memories that need to be addressed? Things that happened between you and your parents? Or something they don't know about? Think about what you would do or say if you *did* care and were *less* angry.

When you journal, write down every single reason or thing that makes you angry about not fitting in. After you do this, take time to engage in a calming activity or get some exercise. Come back when you're in a good space, and pretend that you are reading something from another teen. Does how angry you are feeling fit what you have experienced? If it's a "yes," then have a conversation with your parents about it. If it's a "no," think about what you need to do to let those feelings go and move on. But consider talking with your parents about your feelings anyway.

Q+A 10

Q: My friend often posts comments on my pictures on social media about me that look fine to others, but I know these comments are passive-aggressive because she is hinting at things I told her in private. I called her out on social media, and now all my other friends are mad at me and say I am too aggressive. But how else am I supposed to deal with her?

A: Communication can be so tricky. The further away we get from face-to-face communication, the trickier it gets. Sometimes we can read into something that is not there. This is not me doubting your experience of your friend, but it is something to keep in mind when communicating.

Calling someone out in public on social media is not an ideal way to handle conflict. It is more healthy to have a conversation with the person directly. Dealing with it privately shifts the other person's reaction and allows them to be more receptive—it also prevents them from reading something that is not there. There could also be something deeper going on. Is there some old hurt that needs to be addressed? Maybe your friend is mad about something you did and you don't know?

A helpful question to start the conversation can be "Is everything okay between us?"

During the talk, using "I" statements can be really helpful. The importance of "I" statements is to share how you feel without blaming the other person so you can make a request setting a boundary for the future.

Here is the setup for an "I" statement:

I feel _____ when _____ _____.

In the future, _____.

For example, "I feel hurt when I post a selfie and you make a comment about how my hair looks. In the future, could you not say negative comments on social media posts and instead direct message me?"

Q+A 11

Q: I don't feel understood by my mother. She never supports me and doesn't believe me when I tell her my teachers are lying. She always wants to talk about my grades, but I just end up screaming at her. What should I do?

A: It's really frustrating when teens are struggling with school, and it feels like their parents don't believe them and are taking the side of teachers.

Sometimes the things we've done in the past impact whether someone believes us now. Have you talked with your mother about what would need to happen for her to believe you? Is there some behavior that she needs to see shifted first?

Sometimes parents simply do not believe us and may be struggling with their own challenges. In that case, all you can do is make your best effort to communicate. In the end, the only real control you have is over yourself.

It's tough to talk about uncomfortable topics. But if these topics, such as failing grades, aren't discussed and a plan is not created, nothing will change. The cycle will continue and everyone will be miserable.

When preparing for a difficult conversation, use these journal prompts to think through anything you're worried about and prepare for the conversation.

1. What is your goal with this conversation? _____

_____

2. What's your worst fear about the conversation? _____

_____

3. Is your fear true or likely? _____

_____

4. What do you need to feel confident in the conversation? _____

_____

5. Which is worse: the discomfort of having the conversation or the consequences of not having it? _____

_____

Use these reminders for a successful conversation.

1. Listen first without reacting.

2. Be clear and use fewer words.

3. Put yourself into the other person's shoes.

4. If tension gets high, agree to take a five-minute break and then come back.

5. Be okay with a difference of opinions.

6. Do something to release tension afterward (such as the Pull and Release exercise [page 44]).

7. Schedule a follow-up conversation if needed.

Q+A 12

Q: I get angry so easily and then it takes me forever to feel better. Even if I have something fun to do, like going to a party or hanging out with my friends, I just can't seem to let my anger go. How can I stop this?

A: It can be hard to shake the sensation of anger sometimes. In part 1, we talked about how the body releases chemicals when angry, and they don't just leave your body once you are calm (page 19). Your muscles might be more tense as well. On top of this, people can often be fixated on what occurred, focusing on either what they did (or didn't do) or what the other person did.

First, you'll want to do something physical to release the anger from your body. You can go for a run or do some other exercise. If you need ideas, review the Level Up exercise (page 36) and look at some of the active ways to release anger.

After the anger is released, you may still be hyper-focused on what happened. If so, think about if it makes sense to be angry over what occurred. On a scale of 0 to 10, how important is this event in the big picture? If something is important, such as being higher than an 8, then you'll want to take a *healthy* action. For example, if it's a person who has caused your angry feelings, try talking with them or setting a boundary (Q&A 10 [page 91]).

A 0 on the scale would be something that doesn't matter, like having to decide if you want ketchup or mayonnaise on a sandwich. A 1 might be planning to go to your favorite restaurant all week and then getting there and finding that it is closed. Something above an 8 would be something very intense, such as a breakup or life-altering event.

When we're able to realize that something might not be as important in the grand scheme of things as it feels in the moment, it can give us perspective and can make us feel not so angry.

Q+A 13

Q: I often use my words to hurt other people's feelings. Sometimes I do it on purpose, and other times it just comes out. I feel like I just can't help it. Is there any way to control this?

A: Sometimes it can be really hard to take a moment before saying something. However, learning this skill can be super valuable. The next time you find yourself in a situation where you want to say something on impulse, follow these five steps:

1. Take a breath.

2. Make a kind or neutral facial expression.

3. Count to three before you say anything.

4. Talk slowly so you can think about what you're saying.

5. If you need more time to think about what you want to say, let the other person know. Tell them you'll respond later.

One thing to think about in these instances: Are there certain triggers that you notice when you are saying something mean? Flip to the Anger Triggers exercise (page 22) and review the list of triggers. Think about the last time you used your words to hurt others. Was your action caused by a trigger on that list? If so, notice if you are having specific negative thoughts about yourself in these situations. Then create some other, different thoughts to address what has occurred, just like in the Inner Critic exercise (page 60). Also, consider sharing how you are feeling with the person if you think you need to set specific boundaries. Don't forget to apologize if necessary.

Q+A 14

Q: My friend started dating a girl I like, and it makes me so angry. She agreed to not do this, but when I was away on vacation they started dating. She's supposed to be my best friend. I never want to talk to her again and I want her to feel bad about what she did. What should I do?

A: I can see how you'd feel angry and hurt by this. Following are a few questions to consider when deciding what to do next.

1. How are you are going to feel if you end the friendship??

_____

_____

2. Will the satisfaction you might experience be worth the guilt that might come?

_____

_____

3. Is it worth losing your friendship over this?

_____

_____

When making decisions like this, doing what's called a *cost–benefit analysis* can be helpful. It can help you see if the cost (the negative or disadvantage) of the behavior is worth the benefit.

For example, if your thought is that you must stop talking to your friend to feel better, write down what the advantages are (for example, "I'll feel like I have control over the situation") versus the disadvantages (for example, "I'll feel guilty for hurting my friend and I'll miss them"). By doing this, you will often find that one side outweighs the other one, and this will help you decide.

The next time you're facing a situation where you want to act on your anger, use the following chart to create your own cost–benefit analysis. Make sure you are calm and not angry when you complete the chart.

ADVANTAGE(S)	DISADVANTAGE(S)

After you fill out the chart, take a break to give your mind some time to settle. Come back later to look at the chart and see if there is anything you want to add or take off. Then see what it looks like. Is there a clear winner? If so, then this might be the choice you want to make. If it's even, I would recommend talking with someone you trust to get their thoughts.

Q+A 15

Q: I don't have any of the things my friends have. I never get the new gaming console, shoes, summer vacation, and other things that my friends get. How can I not be angry about this when it feels so unfair?

A: We live in a society where it is really easy to compare ourselves to others. On social media, most people post only positive things, like cool items they get or activities they do. This can make others who don't feel great or don't have these items or experiences feel bad about themselves.

Something that can be helpful in these situations is to create a gratitude journal. Every day, sit down and write or draw three or more things that you are grateful for, no matter how small they are. They could be as simple as getting a good grade, sleeping in a warm bed, or having your dog greet you after school or as big as a gift or a life-changing experience.

You might be surprised by how many things there really are in your life to feel good about.

This gratitude journal will do a few things. First, it will remind you that no matter what is happening, there is usually something you can be thankful for. Second, it will help you shift away from negative thinking or envy to more positive ways of thinking.

Q+A 16

Q: My best friend is so annoying sometimes. She keeps getting angry at me for not answering her text messages. I understand communication is important, but she texts so often. I then say rude or hurtful things to her to get her off my back, and we get into a fight. What should I do?

A: Friendships are HARD, at any age. There are so many ways for communication to go sideways. And it feels so complicated when someone is really important to us.

Actually, using the acronym of HARD can remind us what to do in these situations. By remembering an acronym, it helps on two levels: On one end, it helps us remember multiple steps by recalling the letters of a word, and on the other end, it takes us away from our emotions and gets us in our head, which can distract us enough to begin calming our body down a little and thinking more clearly.

When you find yourself in a heated conversation in the moment, think of HARD:

H: Hang back
Don't respond right away. Take some time and then respond.

A: Allow space
Think about what has occurred and set boundaries that might be necessary. (For example, *I feel upset that I can't always talk or text when you want me to. I can't text you after dinner because I have to do my homework.*)

R: Repair
Apologize if you said something you wish you hadn't. Let her know that you care about her and consider if there is something else that needs to be said to repair the relationship.

D: Determine a plan
Create a plan for yourself on how to respond to different triggers, what to do if you lose your cool, and how to continue to set boundaries if needed.

Think about an experience you've had in the past. How could you have responded using HARD?

Q+A 17

Q: Life is so boring sometimes. I know this may sound weird, but it makes me so angry. I grew up expecting all the fun things that I saw teens doing on TV and online to happen to me. I end up taking my frustration out on my family, especially my little brother, who often bugs me and wants to spend time with me. Is there a cure for boredom? Can I do something to feel less frustrated by it?

A: Life is not always super fast-paced with tons of excitement, even for adults. In reality, there are moments of excitement along with many regular, more mundane moments. It's easy to think about what we don't have as opposed to what we do have. When we hyper-focus on what we don't have, we run the risk of getting stuck in one of the thinking conundrums from the Thinking Conundrums exercise (page 29).

Now that you know this happens, you can plan for what to do. Create a list of activities that you enjoy. Keep that list handy for those moments when you might be bored or hitting a brick wall with what to do.

I recommend listing at least 25 things to do. Be as specific as possible. For example, instead of saying "play a game," write each game you might want to play. If you're into cooking, write down 10 recipes you want to make. If you're into exercise, create a variety of fitness goals and work on them when you're bored. Or learn a new skill because one thing is true: In this day and age, there is such easy access to ways of learning new things and so many activities out there. Let your imagination run wild and go and do.

Fun Activities

Q+A 18

Q: No one understands me. It makes me want to go to my room, slam the door, and never leave. When I do talk with people, I know I'm not really fun to be around and often come off as rude. Why do I feel this way?

A: Not feeling understood can be really painful. I sometimes wonder, what does it mean to be understood? Often this means feeling seen or heard. In therapy, I can support people with experiences I have never had, and they still feel like I understand them. This makes me think that it is possible for those around you to understand you even if you don't feel like they do.

Here are three questions to consider.

1. Do you feel like you understand yourself? Why or why not? _____

_____

_____

_____

2. How would you know that you have been understood? _____

_____

_____

_____

3. What are you trying to tell people or make them understand? _____

_____

_____

_____

Here are several tips that could help you feel more understood by those around you.

1. Make sure you speak up and try to explain what is happening.

2. Consider that your friends are teens just like you and might not understand because they may lack skills or be going through their own stuff.

3. Check to see if there is something inside you that's making you not want to allow someone to understand you.

4. Recognize that only you can completely understand yourself and expecting this from someone else might set them up to fail and for you to not feel connected with others. Small connections are valuable, so seek out little ways that you can get on the same wavelength by sharing and listening about likes, dislikes, dreams, and ideas.

Q+A 19

Q: I do so much around my house. I babysit, do the dishes, help make dinner, and even pick up my siblings. Sometimes I have to change my plans with my friends because of my responsibilities. I don't complain or anything. But it feels like no one cares. This makes me angry, and so I find myself being passive-aggressive. And this is the only thing my family notices and then they complain about it, which makes me even more angry. Can I do anything to change this?

A: It sounds like you're not feeling appreciated by your family. As humans, we like to hear positive things about ourselves, especially when we have done something nice. And sometimes we don't want to do the nice thing or be nice to the person if we don't feel like others appreciate what we're doing.

The cool thing is that sometimes by simply understanding our own emotions and why we are feeling this way, we start to feel better.

Sometimes people show love and appreciation in different ways. It may be through actions, words, or even spending time together. When you consider those three different categories, could you see ways that your family might be appreciating you that you might not have seen before?

If not, ask to have a conversation with them. Sharing with your family how you are feeling will help them understand your feelings and allow them to respond from their viewpoint. Talking things through will probably result in you feeling more appreciated and less angry at them. If needed, refer back to the questions in Q&A 11 (page 92) for tips for a productive conversation.

Q+A 20

Q: I am in a group chat that has a few people who just really annoy me, and I wish they were not in the chat. I often respond right away when they say something I don't like. My mom thinks that I should wait before I respond, but what's the point?

A: Anytime we respond right away, whether we mean to or not, we can come across to others in a less-than-great way. From the other person's point of view, it might not seem like we put much consideration into what we were saying, which could increase the likelihood that they do not feel understood.

This might be even more intensified if we don't like the person, as they most likely have already sensed this. Unfortunately, there will always be people you do not like that much in life, but it's important to treat them how you'd want to be treated by others. You can dislike someone but still be respectful to them.

Communication that's not in person can be really challenging. We or the person on the other end might assume a text has a tone that is not there, or due to autocorrect or simply an error, what we are trying to say or understand from someone else can be easily misunderstood.

In the beginning of the book, we discussed fight-or-flight responses (page 2). When you read a text message that triggers anger in the moment and you respond right away, this is a fight response. When you do this, you might be responding without your whole brain chiming in due to being in fight response, and as a result, you are more likely to say something you wish you hadn't.

Before you respond to a text that frustrates you, sleep on it. When you respond right away, you are being impulsive. When you're impulsive, you are more likely to engage in a behavior that you might regret. By delaying your response, you have more time to think about it, and often the initial charge of anger will be gone.

Here are a few good questions to ask yourself before you respond to something upsetting. Feel free to use the write-in lines to journal about a specific experience.

1. Is this response needed? _____

2. What am I hoping to get out of this response? _____

   _____

3. Is this response helpful or hurtful? _____

Q+A 21

Q: My siblings and I often fight. Once or twice we've thrown things at one another. I know it's not healthy, but I am unsure how to change our behavior. What should we do?

A: It's great that you have realized that this is not healthy. That is the first step to making changes. It can be common for us to express our anger more intensely at those we love, such as our parents, friends, and siblings. This is in large part due to knowing that they will continue to be there for us and love us. However, the more we do this, the more we learn dysfunctional dynamics and the more we can push people away.

First and foremost, you're right: This does need to shift. Behaviors like these tend to build up if we think they are okay and can lead to serious negative consequences.

Here's what I suggest: Sit down together and plan how to communicate to each other when you're getting upset. When you have this conversation, make sure to stay on the topic. Try not to bring up things from the past and instead focus on creating a plan moving forward. Listen to one another.

Next time you do become upset, make sure to leave and take space instead of engaging in aggressive behaviors. You might just say, "I am going to walk away for a few minutes because I need to calm down. I'll be back so we can talk more calmly."

Q+A 22

Q: It seems like small things just really anger me and they build up. It's like a Jenga tower—when enough things bother me, I explode, and it all tumbles down. My family doesn't understand this and thinks there's something wrong with me. How can I "let the small things go," like people ask me to?

A: The good news is that there are many ways to help with this. The best way is to engage in a relaxing activity as soon as you start to notice that anger is beginning to build up. Letting go of the small things is much easier when you are feeling relaxed and often comes naturally in this state.

One relaxing activity to try is called progressive muscle relaxation. In this exercise, you will be tensing and releasing the different muscles in your body.

1. Get into a comfortable position.

2. Take at least five deep breaths.

3. You can begin with any muscle group you like, but I prefer for people to start at their head and then work their way down their body. Tense up your face muscles for 15 seconds, and then relax them for 15 seconds.

4. Repeat step 3 with your neck, back, left and right arms (one at a time or together), left and right hands (one at a time or together), stomach, glutes (butt muscles), thighs, calves, and then feet muscles.

This exercise can also help when you are trying to fall asleep or in a stressful situation, like before a presentation or when doing something scary.

Additionally, consider journaling about "the small things" you're experiencing to discover what's really happening with this buildup of emotions. Pairing the journaling with the progressive muscle relaxation technique will get you the best results.

Q+A 23

Q: I get so angry that I destroy items that belong to me. This often happens when I am doing something and can't do it just right, such as putting on makeup or doing homework. How do I change this?

A: It may sound simple, but the first thing you will want to do is to take a five-minute break from the task you are doing to do something else. You could get up and drink some water, walk around the block, do some jumping jacks, or watch a funny YouTube video.

Following this, notice if there are any negative thoughts about yourself occurring. With perfectionism, these can be thoughts such as "I am a failure if I am not perfect." And then do a thought battle from Inner Critic (page 60) or a cost–benefit analysis from Q&A 14 (page 96).

Then, before you go back to the task that is frustrating you, try a breathing exercise to relax yourself. One such exercise is called box breathing.

To engage in box breathing, imagine a box like the one shown. You can look at this box or just hold the image in your mind. Imagine breathing up the left side of the box for five seconds. When you are at the top, hold your breath for five seconds, imagining that holding of your breath extending across the entire top of the box. Exhale for five seconds as you go down the right side and then hold it again for five seconds as you go across the bottom from right to left. Breathe around the box five to 10 times in a row.

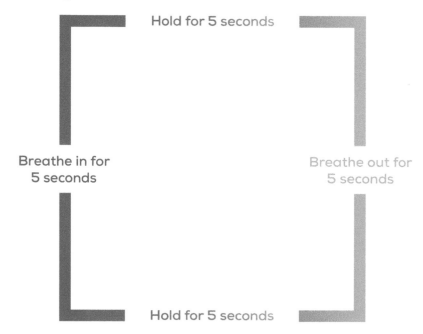

Hold for 5 seconds

Breathe in for 5 seconds

Breathe out for 5 seconds

Hold for 5 seconds

Q+A 24

Q: Sometimes I get so jealous of other people. This happens with friends when they hang out together without me or if I notice two of them are becoming closer than I am with them. Why is this happening, and what should I do about this feeling?

A: Jealousy, like most emotions, can be helpful when used correctly. It's there to tell us that we are feeling threatened, left out, fearful of losing something, or lonely. Sometimes it might be about the current situation. For example, are your friends really ignoring you and leaving you out? Are you feeling lonely because of this? Sometimes it might be about something that happened in the past. Was there an unresolved disagreement that requires a repair? Was something mean said and not addressed?

Often, when we are feeling jealous, there is also a negative belief about ourselves occurring. This could be something like *I cannot keep close friends*, *I am not good enough*, or even *I feel invisible*.

Being able to manage jealousy is important, since too much of it can cause more conflict in all kinds of relationships.

Use jealousy to let you know that something needs to change and that a conversation most likely needs to take place. See page 91 for a reminder on how to start an "I" statement dialogue.

Q+A 25

Q: I have a hard time not getting angry when someone else is angry. It's like the moment I know someone is mad, I begin to get angry, too. Even if they're not mad at me directly, I can feel myself begin to become agitated. What's going on, and how can I stay calm in these situations?

A: This is a really common response to anger. It's hard to be in the presence of someone else who is angry. Sometimes people direct anger at us and blame us. Other times we might wonder if we did something to make the other person angry, even if they are not directing their anger at us. Or we might even pick up on their angry energy and become agitated ourselves.

The best thing to do is not take it personally. People often have stuff going on in their lives that might be causing the anger, and they are unfortunately taking it out on you. In this case, you might need to set a boundary with the person or with yourself. With the person, it might be requesting that they take space when this happens. For yourself, it might be not spending as much time with that person or leaving when they are not able to control their anger.

Two techniques I often recommend when someone is angry are (1) imagine that person as their small child self or a cute and cuddly character or (2) imagine sending them love and compassion, as that's what they are most likely needing in the moment.

YOU'RE ON YOUR WAY

CONGRATULATIONS! You made it through the book. I know that parts of the book might have been easier than others, and you might have had to do some soul searching. But you did it. I hope you feel proud of yourself for accomplishing this first step in your shift in making anger work for you as opposed to against you.

Throughout the book, you learned new information about anger, different causes, what triggers you have, and a variety of ways to release, prevent, and manage your anger.

Moving forward, there is still work to be done. You'll have weeks when you think to yourself, "I've got this!" and other weeks when you will wonder, "What's happening?" and "Why is managing anger so hard?"

With any new skill, the most important thing is to practice. With continued practice of the different skills, you will get better at managing your anger. You'll also notice that doing so becomes easier over time.

Will you make mistakes? Yes, of course. We all do. But that's okay. My hope for you is that instead of feeling like a mistake is a setback or that shifting anger is impossible, you will instead look at the mistake, see what happened, and determine to do it differently in the future.

Make sure to keep the main list that has all your coping skills handy from the Anger Management Plan you created (page 77).

If a skill stops working or if you find one that works better, add it to the list. You're always changing, and so will what works for you.

I am so excited that you are on your way to taming anger and being your best you. I invite you to circle back to the different parts of this book for a refresher whenever you need one, and check out the following resources for videos, books, websites, and podcasts. We never stop learning how to be our best!

RESOURCES FOR TEENS

Videos

Videos showing how to complete exercises from this book can be accessed at HollyFormanPatel.com/anger.

Books

Don't Let Your Emotions Run Your Life for Teens: Dialectical Behavior Therapy Skills for Helping You Manage Mood Swings, Control Angry Outbursts, and Get Along with Others by Sheri Van Dijk

The Ultimate Self-Esteem Workbook for Teens: Overcome Insecurity, Defeat Your Inner Critic, and Live Confidently by Megan MacCutcheon

A Year of Positive Thinking for Teens: Daily Motivation to Beat Stress, Inspire Happiness, and Achieve Your Goals by Katie Hurley

Websites

10 Cool Meditations for Pre-Teens and Teens: DoYou.com/10-cool-meditations-for-pre-teens -and-teens-67578

Mindfulness for Teens: Guided Meditation: MindfulnessForTeens.com/guided-meditations

The Science of Anger: YouTube.com/watch?v=d_5DU5opOFk

Podcasts

Teenager Therapy

Adult-ish

Unstoppable Teen

Hashtags

#angercontrol

#angermangement

Apps

Calm, a mindfulness and sleep app: Calm.com

Daylio, a mood tracking and journal app: Daylio.net

Headspace, a mindfulness and sleep app: Headspace.com

Moodtrack Diary, a mood tracking and journaling app: Moodtrack.com

RESOURCES FOR PARENTS

Books

Brainstorm: The Power and Purpose of the Teenage Brain by Daniel J. Siegel

The Cognitive Behavioral Workbook for Anger: A Step-by-Step Program for Success by William J. Knaus

The Self-Driven Child: The Science and Sense of Giving Your Kids More Control over Their Lives by William Stixrud and Ned Johnson

The Teenage Brain: A Neuroscientist's Survival Guide to Raising Adolescents and Young Adults by Frances E. Jensen and Amy Ellis Nutt

Websites

8 Ways to Teach Teens Anger Management Skills: VeryWellFamily.com/teach-teens-anger -management-skills-2609114

20 Reasons Why Your Teens Get Mad at You: HuffPost.com/entry/20-reasons-why-your -teens-get-mad-at-you_b_9402664

Anger and Anger Management for Parents: RaisingChildren.net.au/guides/first-1000-days /looking-after-yourself/anger-management-for-parents

Anger Is Your Ally: A Mindful Approach to Anger: YouTube.com/watch?v=sbVBsrNnBy8

Dr. Dan Siegel's Hand Model of the Brain: YouTube.com/watch?v=f-m2YcdMdFw

Help for Parents of Troubled Teens: HelpGuide.org/articles/parenting-family/helping -troubled-teens.htm

How Parents Can Help Troubled Teens Cope with Anger: VeryWellMind.com/what-parents -can-do-to-help-teens-cope-with-anger-2610347

How to Handle Your Anger at Your Child: PsychologyToday.com/us/blog/peaceful-parents -happy-kids/201605/how-handle-your-anger-your-child

Parenting an Angry Explosive Teen: What You Should—and Shouldn't—Do: EmpoweringParents .com/article/parenting-an-angry-explosive-teen-what-you-should-and-shouldnt-do

Psychology Today's Therapist Directory: PsychologyToday.com/us/therapists

Podcasts

Mighty Parenting, Raising Teens, Parenting Young Adults

Talking to Teens: Expert Tips for Parenting Teenagers

Your Teen with Sue and Steph

REFERENCES

Alia-Klein, Nelly, Gabriela Gan, Gadi Gilam, Jessica Bezek, Antonio Bruno, Thomas F. Denson, Talma Hendler, et al. "The Feeling of Anger; From Brain Networks to Linguistic Expressions." *Neuroscience & Biobehavioral Reviews* 108 (January 2020): 480–497. sciencedirect.com /science/article/pii/S0149763419302167.

American Psychological Association. "Controlling Anger Before It Controls You." Last modified 2005. apa.org/topics/anger/control.

Hendricks, LaVelle, Sam Bore, Dean Aslinia, and Guy Morriss. "The Effects of Anger on the Brain." *National Forum Journal of Counseling and Addiction* 2, no. 1 (2013).

Kay, Cameron Stuart and Leike Braadbaart. "In Defense of Anger: An Evolutionary Necessity and Its Contemporary Applicability." *The Inquisitive Mind* 3, no. 33 (March 17). in-mind.org /article/in-defense-of-anger-an-evolutionary-necessity-and-its-contemporary-applicability.

Leahy, Robert L. *Cognitive Therapy Techniques: A Practitioner's Guide.* New York: The Guilford Press, 2003.

Lisitsa, Ellie. "The Four Horsemen: Criticism, Contempt, Defensiveness, and Stonewalling." Last modified April 23, 2013. gottman.com/blog/the-four-horsemen-recognizing-criticism -contempt-defensiveness-and-stonewalling.

Oolup, Craig, Jason Brown, Elizabeth Nowicki, and Danielle Aziz. "The Emotional Experience and Expression of Anger: Children's Perspective." *Child and Adolescent Social Work Journal* 33 (2016): 279–292.

Shapiro, Francine. *Eye Movement Desensitization and Reprocessing (EMDR) Therapy.* New York: The Guilford Press, 2018.

INDEX

ACKNOWLEDGMENTS

Thank you to all the teens and preteens who I have worked with over the years who have allowed me to witness the amazing shifts you've made in your relationship with anger. You rock.

ABOUT THE AUTHOR

Holly Forman-Patel, MA, LMFT, LPCC, is a licensed marriage and family therapist and licensed professional clinical counselor. She has worked with children and teens throughout her career in different capacities and settings, including as a preschool teacher, as a therapist in the Berkeley school system, and, for more than a decade, as a practitioner in her therapy private practice.

Her specialties include not only working with anger but also working with children, teens, and adults recovering from trauma. She is versed in Eye Movement Desensitization and Reprocessing (EMDR) Therapy, a proven way to support people who have experienced traumatic events, and assists in facilitation at trainings for other therapists learning EMDR.

She recently moved from the San Francisco Bay area to Dallas, Texas. When she is not working, she enjoys cooking, gardening, and anything involving comedy.